A TREATISE ON

Buddhist Philosophy of Abhidhamma

Bibliotheca Indo-Buddhica Series

General Editor

SUNIL GUPTA

BIBLIOTHECA INDO-BUDDHICA SERIES NO. 56

A TREATISE ON

Buddhist Philosophy of Abhidhamma

By

Dr. C.L.A. De SILVA

Consciousness, Mental Properties and Particular Concomitants in Consciousness

Revised by The Venerable Narada Thero

Sri Satguru Publications

A Division of

Indian Books Centre

Delhi - India

Published by:
Sri Satguru Publications
Indological and Oriental Publishers
A Division of
Indian Books Centre
40/5, Shakti Nagar,
Delhi-110007
(INDIA)

First Edition : Colombo, 1937

Reprint Edition : Delhi, 1988, 1997

ISBN : 81-7030-174-2

Published by Sunil Gupta, for Sri Satguru Publications, a division of, Indian Books Centre, 40/5, Shakti Nagar, Delhi-110007, India and Printed at Computer Codes, Delhi-110009.

PRINTED IN INDIA

This Book is Dedicated

to

The Memory

of

My Aunt

Mrs. A. E. De Silva (snr.)

CONTENTS.

CHAPTER VI.

PART II.

CHAPTER VII.

Page

CHAPTER VIII.

CHAPTER IX.

CHAPTER X.

CHAPTER XI

CHAPTER XII.

PART III.

CHAPTER XIII.

NAMŌ TASSA BHAGAVATŌ ARAHATŌ SAMMĀ SAMBUDDHASSA.

PREFACE.

By reason of the Oriental languages, such as Sinhalese and Pali, being not subjects included in the curriculum of most schools till recently, the average educated Buddhist of the present day appears to be in total ignorance of Buddhist philosophy in particular and The Buddha Dhamma in general. The more fortunate ones who take a keen interest in the study of the doctrine and thirst for knowledge have no other alternative but to resort to publications of The Pali Text Society. It is unfortunate that the editor Mrs. Rhys Davids, who has such scholastic attainments as to render absolutely correct translations from the original Pali and commentaries, very often contorts facts and misrepresents the doctrine interpolating her views in conformity with The Mahayana Buddhism and from the point of view of Christianity. As a result of this, the student who reads Pali Text Society publications, although he gathers knowledge of the doctrine, is likely to go astray.

Out of compassion to my unfortunate brothers and sisters I make a bold attempt to undertake the extremely difficult task of writing a treatise on Buddhist Philosophy or Abhidhamma Pitaka. It will be seen that The Abhidhamma Attha Sangaha written by The Venerable Anuruddha Thēro is being utilized as the basis for this work. In this exposition the seven books on Abhidamma Pitaka, their commentaries and sub-commentaries will be consulted to such an extent only as to avoid the two extremes and follow the middle path.

I have often heard from some Bhikkhus and laymen that a knowledge of the Abhidhamma is not absolutely necessary for one to reach the goal he is striving for. I think otherwise; and the greater the knowledge he possesses of this abstruse philosophy, the more easily and sooner will he be able to eradicate the erroneous views of a personal entity—ego—theory of soul or *atman* and cast away the sixteen types of doubt which impede one's spiritual progress, and contemplate on the three salient marks or characteristics from the knowledge of things in general as composite up to the knowledge which is qualification for the path and gain emancipation.

A thorough comprehension of the analysis of mind and body with reference to their respective features, essential properties, resulting phenomena and proximate causes and a comprehension of the causal relations of mind and body, *viz* the Law of dependent origination and the system of correlation are absolutely necessary for The Purity of views and Purity of escaping from doubt when one practices exercises in Insight.

Therefore I sincerely hope that all my brothers and sisters will take a keen and active interest in this compilation, which, I expect, would tend to dispel erroneous perceptions, ideas, and views that one is obsessed with, and help one to practise exercises in calm and insight which will ultimately lead one to Nibbāna, through one of the channels of emancipation.

Before concluding I must express my great indebtedness to The Venerable Pelene Siri Vajiragnana Maha Nayaka Thero and his pupil Venerable Narada Thēro for the great assistance rendered in going through the proofs and making necessary corrections.

C. L. A. De SILVA,
Author.

PRIYAWIMANA,
NEGOMBO.
24TH MAY, 1937.

INTRODUCTION.

The Buddha Dhamma consists of three sections *viz* Sutta Pitaka, Abhidhamma Pitaka and Vinaya Pitaka. The Abhidhamma Pitaka consists of seven books *viz*, Dhammasangani Vibhanga, Dhātukathā, Puggalapaññatti, Kathāwatthu, Yamaka and Paṭṭhāna, which are known as the seven Prakaranas.

At the first Council held immediately after the Lord's Parinibbāna by 500 Arahats headed by The Venerable Mahakassapa Thera, Upali Thera and Ananda Thera, the Three Pitakas in the Pali language, were duly recited and rehearsed. In like manner these were recited and rehearsed at the two subsequent Councils held 100 years and 236 years respectively after the Parinibbāna under the leadership of Venerable Yasa and Moggaliputta Tissa Theras.

Not long after the third Council which was held in the reign of Dhammāsoka, his son The Venerable Mahinda Maha Thera brought into Ceylon The Pali Commentaries. Upon the admission of the Sinhalese Bhikkhus to the Buddhist Order, Arittha Thera and others of the Sinhalese race translated the Pali Commentaries into the Sinhalese language and had them all committed to memory. Later, at Alulena, at present known as Aluvihāra in the Matale district 500 Arahats under the auspices of the great King Vatta Gāmini Abhaya, held a convocation and committed the Three Pitakas and the Commentaries to writing.

As time went on, there came to exist several Sinhalese Commentaries called Mahapaccariya Aṭṭhakathā so named because it was composed inside a large raft, Kurundi Aṭṭhakathā by reason of its having been composed in a place called Kurundivelli, and Mahā Aṭṭhakathā following the fact that the copy was made at the Mahā Vihāra. There was also a Commentary written in the Andra language known as Andaṭṭhakathā.

In course of time The Bhikkhus in India formed themselves into seventeen Nikāyas or factions. As a result the original Pāli Commentaries which had come down from mouth to mouth got mixed up with the different views held by these different factions. In consequence thereof, as well as by reason of the non-existence of the texts in writing and also through diverse other causes, The Holy Text fell into decline in India. At the same time, however, it flourished in Ceylon where The Mahā Vihāra Bhikkus—the pupillary descendants of The Venerable Mahinda Mahā Thera—remained orthodox. Amongst them the Three Pitakas with their Sinhalese Commentaries were also available in book form. There were also learned preceptors amongst them highly competent to render correct exposition of the doctrine and to make a clean sweep of the heresies introduced by the Bhikkhus of Dēnanakha and Bhagirinakha sects and by those who held the heretical views known as Vaitulyavāda, Vajiriyavāda and Ratnakuṭavāda.

At this period The Venerable Buddhaghōsa Mahā Thera, a Brahmin born in Northern India, studied the Ḋhamma and established his competence among his country folk. Later he travelled to Ceylon, and under the guidance of the preceptor Venerable Sanghapāla Thera, he studied the Three Pitakas in accordance with the instructions of The Mahā Vihāra fraternity, and under the guidance of the preceptor Venerable Buddhamitta Thera, he studied the Sinhalese Commentaries, The Mahā Aṭṭhakathā Mahāpaccariya, Aṭṭhakathā and Kurundiya Aṭṭhakathā Then he expressed the object of his visit to Ceylon, namely, to translate the Sinhalese Commentaries into Pāli.

Thereupon the Sinhalese preceptors, who were versed in the three Pitakas and were also able to recite the same from memory, desired to test the fitness of The Venerable Buddhaghosa, and requested him to write a commentary on a single stanza which occurs in the Devatā-Sanyuttaka of the Sanyutta Nikāya, namely :—

සීලෙ පතිඨාය නරො සපඤ්ඤො
චිතතං පඤ්ඤඤ්ච භාවයං
ආතාපි නිපකො භිකඛු
සො ඉමං විජටයෙ ජටං

Sīlē patiṭṭhāya narō sapaññō
Cittañ paññanca bhāvayañ
Ātāpi nipakō bhikkhu
So imañ vijatayējatañ

The man discreet, on virtue planted firm,
In intellect and intuition trained,
The brother ardent and discriminant,
'Tis he may from this tangle disembroil.

In response to this invitation, Buddhaghosa compiled The Visuddhi Magga with material picked up by careful research into the entire region of the Three Pitakas.

This able exposition of the Dhamma provided in itself ample testimony as to his fitness and ability for the task. Therefore the great Theras of Ceylon granted him permission to translate the Sinhalese Commentaries into Pāli. The trust reposed in The Venerable Buddhaghosa was only honoured by him by faithfully following the rules of the Mahā Vihāra Fraternity, and accurately converting into the Pāli language the Sinhalese Commentaries of the three Piṭakas with the exception of a of The Kuddhaka Nikāya.

The Commentary called the Samantāpāsādika in the Vinaya Piṭaka was compiled according to the author Venerable Buddhaghosa, upon the invitation of the Venerable Buddhasiri Thēro, while residing at the great mansion Mahāpāya, built and placed at the disposal of The Venerable Buddhaghosa by one Mahanigama Swāmi, a Sinhalese Chief, within the great college associated by the Bhikkhus of the highest and purest discipline, situated to the south of Sri Mahā Bōdhi Vihāra in Mahāmēgha Park at Anuradhapura, in the twentieth year of the reign of King Siriniwāsa of Ceylon. Of the rest of the translations two appear to have been written by him while in residence in the same monastery. Upon the invitation of a Venerable Thera called Culla Buddhaghosa he wrote the Commentaries Atthasālini, Sammōhavinōdanī and Pancappakarana Aṭṭhakathā on the Abhidamma Piṭaka. Various other Theras of eminence were instrumental in getting The Venerable Buddhaghosa to write the Commentaries Sumangala-Vilāsani on the Dīgha Nikāya, Papanchasūdanī on The Majjhima Nikāya, Manōrathapūranī on The Anguttara Nikāya, Sāratthapakāsini on Sanyutta Nikāya, Dhammapadaṭṭhakathā on The Dhammapada, Jātakaṭṭhakathā on the Jātaka series and Kankhā Vitarani on the Ubhaya-Pātimokha.

The Maha Thera Venerable Ananda of the Māha Vihāra who was versed in the Three Pitakas and their Commentaries compiled a sub-commentary by the name Mūlaṭika for all the Commentaries of The Abhidhamma Piṭaka. The Venerable Dhammapāla Thera, a commentator who lived in Baḍaratirtha Vihāra in Nagapaṭṭana now known as Nagapatam, came over to Ceylon and compiled Commentaries on the books of The Khuddaka Nikāya not commented on by The Venerable Buddhaghosa and this Venerable Dhammapāla Thera also wrote an Anutika (A sub-commentary) on the aforesaid Mūlatika. One more sub-commentary by the name Madhu Sāratthadīpani or Madhutika on the same Mūlatika was compiled by The Venerable Ananda Thera of Maharama in the city of Hansawati in the Rāmañña country. A Pali glossary was also written for the same book by one Venerable Nānakithi Thera who lived in a Vihara known as Panasarama in the same country. A Burmese paraphrase was added by a Burmese Thera. Several other Theras also wrote glossaries and explanatory annotations for the same book.

During the Sitāwaka period, the line of The Māha Vihāra Fraternity having come to extinction, the apprehension of even the accurate meaning of certain words gradually declined, less to say anything of the study of the many commentaries. By reason of there being no Sinhalese work on the subject, The Sammohavinōdani, the Commentary on the Vibhangappakarana, the second book of Abhidhamma Piṭaka got out of reach of the beginners. Similarly works of the sort of Mulātika too fell into disuse.

CONTEMPLATION OF THE ABHIDHAMMA PITAKA.

Our Lord, the Omniscient, The Exalted Master, in the fourth week after attaining Enlightenment began to contemplate and review The Dhamma he had realized, being seated in the golden dwelling, placed at his disposal by the Dēvas by their Iddhi powers. When The Lord began to review The Abhidhamma Piṭaka, it was not till he delved into the depths of the most subtlē and abstruse Dhamma in the Mahā Paṭṭhāna which deals with the twenty four causal circumstances or relations that invariably take place in any phenomenon or event or thing, that he experienced pleasurable interest amounting to rapture. The psychological pleasure and happy feelings were so great that, as a result of the brilliant and sparkling condition of the blood associated with the heart-base, which occured in the consciousness accompanied by joy and connected with knowledge, that the six-coloured rays emanated from the body downwards penetrating the earth, water and air and upwards as far as the sphere of neither Perception nor No Perception and in the other eight directions endlessly as the four great essentials constitute the elements of the world. How this extraordinary and almost incredible phenomenon took place is explained in this manner that the sparkling and brilliant material qualities originating from mind occasioned a similar condition of the skin by their diffusion. From that cause the colour of the visible object which was occasioned by mind and physical environment, stood without the slightest movement covering a space of almost one hundred and twenty feet.

PREACHING OF ABHIDAMMA TO THE DEVAS

The Tathāgata, whose compassion to all living beings alike was no less than the wisdom and insight he had acquired by practising the ten Pāramitās for no less a period than four Asankheyya (incalculable) Kappas and another lakh of Kappas (aeons) since the proclamation by the Lord Deepankara that the ascetic Sumedha would attain enlightenment and be known as Gautama Buddha, in the seventh year of Buddhahood performed the "twin miracle" near the foot of the mango tree at Gandamba so called because it was planted by the gardener Ganda, not far away from Sāvatti, when five hundred men who in their previous existence were bats who had zealously listened to the recital and rehearsal of The Abhidhamma by two brothers of the Sangha, decided to become pupils of Sāriputta and at a later stage were the first to learn without much difficulty all the Dhamma embodied in the seven books or Prakaranas of The Abhidhamma. The reason for performing the "Twin Miracle" by The Lord was to dispel erroneous views and ideas that the Non-Arahants such as Niganṭha Nāthaputta and others had of themselves and with a view to conclusively proving that The Lord had all the attributes of a Buddha. The huge assembly present incidentally acquired great merit and thereafter his followers both the brothers and the laymen demonstrated greater zeal and faith and strenuously followed the Eight Fold Noble Path to attain Nibbāna. The Enlightened one then out of compassion to the Dēvas and Brahmas repaired to the Tāvatingsa Dēvalōka (Heaven of The Thirty Three Gods) in three steps by Iddhi and was seated in the Pāndukambala Sailāsana (Sakra's rock seat) near the foot of the Pāricchattaka tree where he preached The Abhidhamma for three full months to his deceased mother, who is now born as Santhushita Dēva, and other Dēvas and Brahmas who had assembled from the ten thousand worlds, in detail with the hope of making them realize the Four Ariyan Truths, for which a knowledge of Abhidhamma is absolutely necessary, for the subject deals in the highest and ultimate sense of things springing into being as facts as abstracted from or divested of names.

PREACHING OF ABHIDHAMMA IN THE WORLD OF MEN.

The Buddha daily visited Uturukuru Dīpa for the purpose of obtaining his mid-day meals and partook of his meals near Anotattha lake in Himalaya and during the period of rest he took at Handunvanaya, The Venerable Sariputta daily came to attend to the necessary requirements.

Thereafter Māthikā or the headings of the discourses preached to the Dēvas were intimated to The Venerable Sāriputta Māhā Thera, who in turn preached The Abhidhamma in detail beginning from Dhammasangini and ending in The Mahā Paṭṭhāna to his five hundred disciples. By reason of the fact that these disciples in a previous existence, even as bats, had the fortune of hearing the recital and rehearsal of The Abhidhamma by two Bhikkhus and by doing such moral acts as were conducive to the acquirement of knowledge, wisdom, intellect and insight in the round of births, these disciples with the greatest ease mastered the full Abhidhamma Piṭaka and were able to recite same from beginning till end. From that time onwards the Abhidhamma was learnt by the pupillary descendants till the time of the Arahants Upaliya, Dasakaya, Sunakaya, Siggavaya and Moggalliputta Tissa etc. It was rehearsed and recited at the three convocations held under the leadership of Māhā Kassappa, Yasa and Moggaliputta Tissa, and was preserved in its pristine purity in Dambadiva.

INTRODUCTION OF ABHIDHAMMA TO CEYLON.

It was in the 237th year after The Lord's attainment of Pari Nibbāna during the reign of Dēvānampiya Tissa that Abhidamma was first introduced into Ceylon by The Venerable Mahinda Maha Thera, *vide*., introduction pages 1 to 4.

REINTRODUCTION OF ABHIDHAMMA TO DAMBADIVA FROM CEYLON.

The Venerable Uttara Jeeva Maha Thera of Arimaddana in Burma visited Ceylon together with several other Bhikkhus including Chappada Sāmanēra for the purpose of worshipping the different shrines. Having worshipped they went back to Burma, leaving Chappada Sāmanēra under the protection of the Principal of The Sri Sangha Bodhi Wijayabāhu Pirivena in Jayawārdenepura and The Venerable Totagamuwe Siri Rāhula Sangharajah Maha Thera who had a complete mastery of six languages. Chappada Sāmanēra resided in the said Pirivena and learnt the Text Commentaries and sub-commentaries according to the teachings of Thera-vada under The Venerable Totagamuwe Sri Rāhula Sangharajah who had completely mastered the Three Piṭakas. The Sāmanēra associated himself also with The Venerable Vīdagama Maitreiya Mahā Thera who was also versed in the Three Piṭakas and became very learned and clever and in course of time was ordained (obtained Upasampadā) in Kelani Ganga. Later on he was styled Saddhammavara Jothipāla owing to his mastery of the doctrine, and wrote a sub-commentary to The Abhidhammattha Sangaha called Sankhēpavannanā. Having completed his task he went back to Arimaddana in Burma together with three other Maha Theras who had mastered the Three Piṭakas, namely Venerable Thamalittapatuna Sīvalee of Maha Vihara Ananda of Kanchipura and Rāhula of Ceylon.

RESURRECTION OF ABHIDHAMMA IN CEYLON.

Two thousand one hundred and thirty five years after the Lord's attainment of Parinibbāna that is inthe reign of Sitawaka Rājasinha who killed his father, Abhidhamma more or less came into extinction, and the revival of same is due to the untiring efforts of The Pandit M. Dharmaratana. He went to Burma and mastered The Abhidhamma Piṭaka, the commentaries and sub-commentaries from the learned preceptors and became very clever and learned. He was honoured by the title "Buddhasāsana Mahasūra Sēnapati" and was the author of many books which dealt with The Abhidhamma such as Sathwothpatti Viniscaya and Nirwana Vibhāgaya, Paticca Samuppadāya, Visuddhi Magga, Paramartha Sudhanidhiya, Buddhāgama Prathisandhi Deepaniya, Abhidhammattha Sangraha prasnoththaraya Dāna parichchedaya, Sīla parichchēdaya, Bhāvanā parichchēdaya etc.

CONTENTS.

Following The Abhidhammattha Sangaha the subject is dealt with in nine chapters viz :—

(1) Classes of Consciousnesses.
(2) Mental properties (in consciousness).
(3) Particular concomitants in consciousness.
(4) Process of cognition.
(5) Consciousness free from process.
(6) Matter and Nibbāna.
(7) Categories of evil, mixed, of what pertains to Enlightenment and of the whole.
(8) Dependent origination and system of correlation.
(9) Exercises in Calm and Insight.

ABHIDHAMMA MĀTIKĀ.

The Abhidhamma Mātikā is a discourse spoken by our Lord Buddha on the Ethico-Psychological Law called Abhidhamma. This Mātikā forms the text-matter of the whole Abhidhamma Piṭaka.

The Abhidhamma Piṭaka, which consists of seven books, contain discourses of the Arahants, Sāriputta, and Moggaliputta Tissa, having for their text the said Abhidhamma Mātikā spoken by the Lord Buddha.

The Mātikā itself consists of three parts ; namely, Tika-Mātikā, Duka-Mātikā and Suttanta-Mātikā. Of these Tika-Mātikā has twenty two Mātikās or sub-texts and Duka-Mātikā has one hundred Mātikās. These one hundred and twenty two Mātikās are set forth in detail in The Abhidhamma Piṭaka.

The Suttanta-Mātikā has been done by The Venerable Sāriputta Thera by extracting portions from Ēka-nipāta and Dukanipāta in Anguttara Nikāya and from the Sangīti Sutta and Dāsuttara Sutta in Dīgha Nikaya to prevent confusion to students of Abhidhamma in their study of the Sutta Piṭaka, for otherwise the occurrence of these Abhidhamma texts in the Suttas also would cause them some perplexity. Suttanta-Mātikā is still further explained and commented upon in Nikkhēpa Kānda of Dhamma-Sanganipakarana. The Suttanta-Mātikā consists of forty two Mātikās.

Any person who has attained a thorough and critical knowledge of this Mātikā ought to possess a complete knowledge of the concise Abhidhamma Piṭaka.

ABHIDHAMMATTHA SANGAHA AND VIBHĀVINI TIKA.

The Abhidhammattha Sangaha and its Tīka Vibhāvini occupy an unrivalled position as a guide to students of The Abhidhamma or metaphysics of Buddhism. The author of the work was the Venerable Anuruddha, who lived in Tanjore in Southern India, about 953 years after The Buddha attained Parinibbāna and was thus a contemporary of the famous commentator Venerable Buddhaghosa. The same author wrote two other works, the Nāmarūpa-paricchēda and the Paramartha-Vinischaya.

Though various commentaries on The Abhidhammattha Sangaha, written by learned Bhikkus both in Ceylon and in India, are extant, it is universally admitted by learned men in Ceylon and in Burma, that in discrimination none can compare with the Vibhāvini Tīka. The authorship of this commentary is ascribed to The Venerable Sumangala who also wrote The Abhidhammattha Vikāsini a commentary on The Abhidhammavatāra. This Venerable Sumangala was a pupil of The Venerable Maha Sāriputra of the Jētawana Temple in Polonnoruwa, to whom we owe the Sārartha-dīpani, the commentary on the Vinaya.

A student who receives instruction from an Abhidhamma scholar in the Abhidhammattha Sangaha and The Vibhāvini

Tika, will find no difficulty in understanding all the seven books on Abhidhamma and all their commentaries, without the assistance of a tutor.

SYMBOLS SHOWING PRONUNCIATION OF WORDS.

— long as in art

˜ ˜ as in paññā (පඤ්ඤා)

ṭ as in to

t as in thought

bh as in bhavō (භවො)

ch as in cha (ඡ)

c as in citta (චිත්ත)

d as in dosa (දොස)

ṭṭh as in aṭṭhakathā (අට්ඨකථා)

tth as in paramattha (පරමත්ථ)

th as in tathā (තථා)

dh as in aṭṭhadhā (අට්ඨධා)

e as in ēvan (එවං)

u as in uttaran (උත්තරං)

yu as in Sampayuttā (සම්පයුත්තා)

n as in atulan (අතුලං)

jh as in tatramajjhattatā (තත්‍රමජ්ඣත්තතා)

kh as in cakkhu (චක්ඛු)

ph as in phassō (ඵස්සො)

INTRODUCTORY.

NAMŌ TASSA BHAGAVATŌ ARAHATŌ
SAMMĀ SAMBUDDHASSA.

නමො තස්ස භගවතො අරහතො
සම්මා සම්බුද්ධස්ස.

Honour to the Exalted One, the Arahant Buddha Supreme!

Sammā Sambuddha[4] matulan[3] sasaddhamma ganuttaman[2]
Abhivādiya bhāsissan Abhidhammattha sangahan[5]
Tattha vuttābhidhammatthā catuddhā paramatthatō[1]
Chittan[6] cētasikan[7] rūpan[8] nibbānamiti[9] sabbathā

සම්මා සම්බුද්ධමතුලං සසද්ධම්ම ගණුත්තමං
අභිවාදිය භාසිස්සං අභිධම්මත්ථ සඞ්ගහං
තත්ථ වුත්තාභිධම්මත්ථා චතුධා පරමත්ථතො
චිත්තං චෙතසිකං රූපං නිබ්බානමිති සබ්බථා

With reverence I salute the peerless Buddha, the Law of Righteousness, and the Fraternity of supreme worth. Now I will speak in concise summaries of things contained in Abhidhamma-lore. These things are set forth in their ultimate sense as four categories *viz:*

(1) Consciousness (citta) (2) Mental properties (cētasika (3) Matter (rūpa) and (4) Nibbāna.

NOTES 1.

Paramatthatō (පරමත්ථතො) is explained by the Ceylon Commentator as sammutin ṭhapetvā nibbattita paramatthavasēna (සම්මුතිං ඨපෙත්වා නිබ්බත්තිත පරමත්ථවසෙන)—in an abstract or ultimate sense, avoiding the conventional usage.

NOTES 2.

Sasaddhamma ganuttaman (සසද්ධම්ම ගණුත්තමං) is the truth of the Ariyans, that which always remains unchanged in the highest and ultimate sense deserving of honour and reverence, and existing in the mind of only the Ariyans amongst the Dēvas and men.

NOTES 3.

Atulaṅ (අතුලං) having no other equal in respect of morality, concentration, and insight.

NOTES 4.

Sammā Sambuddhan (සම්මාසම්බුද්ධං) is the exalted and enlightened one who realized all states and phenomena both conditioned and unconditioned without any help from others, and solely through the practice of the Ten Pāramitās, on the completion of which he was able to attain Nibbāna through three channels of emanicipation, the three salient marks being realized at the same time.

NOTES 5.

Abhidhammattha sangahan (අභිධම්මත්ථ සඞ්ගහං) is a compendium of philosophy preached by the Enlightened One and embodied in the seven books of Abhidhamma Piṭaka in such analysis as kusala, akusala, aggregates, āyatanas, elements, controlling powers etc.

NOTES 6.

Cittan (චිත්තං) is the aggregate of consciousness which is differentiated into 89 or 121 classes. The function of consciousness, thought, or mind is the discernment of objects. Although there are other correlations, the principle one is the correlation of object, which is responsible for the origination of a state of consciousness, without which a thought can never arise. Consciousness is differentiated into 89 or 121 classes according to the mental properties or concomitants coexistent with it.

NOTES 7.

Cētasikan (චේතසිකං) is a mental state or property. There are in all 52 cētasikas. Feeling or vēdanā is one, Perception or saññā is another. The remaining fifty mental states are collectively called—Sankhārā or volitional activities. There are in all 52 cētasikas or mental concomitants such as contact, feeling, perception, volition, etc. The difference may be illustrated by a mixture containing several ingredients, the water being compared to the citta, (චිත්ත) and cētasikas (චෛතසික) to the several ingredients. Of the two the principal one is the citta (චිත්ත) as in "Manō pubbangamā Dhammā" (මනො පුබ්බඞ්ගමා ධම්මා). Mind is the forerunner of mental states. Mental concomitants cannot arise without consciousness.

Notes. 8.

Rūpaṁ (රූපං) is matter which consists of the four great essentials and the 24 other material qualities derived therefrom. It is so called because it changes by reason of physical conditions as heat and cold. Although there is change in immaterial qualities too, they are not called Rūpa (රූප) as the change is imperceptible, and subtle, and only the material qualities are called rūpa (රූප) because the change is perceptible and apparent in them.

Notes 9.

Nibbāna (නිබ්බාන) is the unconditioned state that becomes the object of the transcendental or supramundane classes of consciousness arising in the four paths and four fruits, Vāna (වාන) is craving Transcending the vana (වාන) is Nirvāna (නිර්වාන) or Nibbāna (නිබ්බාන). It is the extinction or annihilation of the fire of lust, hate, and delusion.

PART I.

Chapter I

Planes of consciousness

Of these, first, consciousness is four-fold *viz*.—

(1) Consciousness as experienced in Kāmalōka[1].

(2) Consciousness as experienced in Rūpalōka.

(3) Consciousness as experienced in Arūpalōka.

(4) Transcendental (supramundane) consciousness.

Note 1.

Consciousness as experienced in Kāmalōka (කාමාවචර චිත්තං) is derived from Kāmē avacaratīti (කාමෙ අවචරතීති) —" that which moves about in, haunts, frequents the Kāmalōka (කාමලොකෙ) and is applied to all classes of Kāma consciousness whether of experience on occasion of sense stimulation or of representative cognition, volition etc. Kāma is either (1) that which desires, Kamētīti Kāmō (කාමෙතීති කාමො) or (2) that which is desired Kāmīyatīti Kāmō (කාමීය තීතිකාමො). The former is subjective and the latter is objective, the latter may refer to the pleasures derived from sense, or to the eieven grades of Kāmalōka life, where such pleasures prevail. These eleven consist of (*a*) the four infra-human forms of existence *viz*, states of misery, the world of Pētas, the world of Asuras, and the animal kingdom. (*b*) in birth as human beings (*c*) and the six heavens of the dēvas. Hence there is no one English equivalent or adequate word for Kāmāvacara (කාමාවචර) or Kāmalōka (කාමලොක). (Therefore the word Kāmalōka and for equivalent reasons, Rūpalōka and Arūpaloka will be retained.).

Summary of Classes of Consciousness.

Classes of Consciousness in the four worlds are as follows :—

As experienced in	Kāmalōka	Worldly	54
do	Rūpalōka	Worldly	15
do	Arūpalōka	Worldly	12
Transcendental or Supramundane			8
			89

(1) Consciousness as experienced in Kāmalōka.

(*a*)	Types of	Immoral Consciousness	12
(*b*)	do	Resultant Consciousness (from past ill deeds)	7
(*c*)	do	Resultant consciousness (from past good deeds)	8
(*d*)	do	Ineffective consciousness (as to future result)	3
		Ahētuka (අහේතුක) unconditioned	18

Consciousness of the Beautiful.

(*a*)	Great types of Moral Consciousness	8
(*b*)	Great type of Moral Consciousness Resultant	8
(*c*)	Great types of Ineffective Consciousness	8

(2) Consciousness as experienced in Rūpalōka.

(*a*)	Moral Consciousness in Jhānas	5
(*b*)	Moral Consciousness Resultants of Jhānas	5
(*c*)	Ineffective Consciousness in Jhānas	5

(3) Consciousness as experienced in Arūpalōka

(*a*)	Moral Consciousness in Arūpa Jhānas	4
(*b*)	Moral Consciousness Resultants of Arūpa Jhānas	4
(*c*)	Ineffective Consciousness in Arūpa Jhānas	4

(4) Transcendental Consciousness (supra-mundane)

(*a*)	Path Consciousness	4
(*b*)	Fruition Consciousness	4
	12+18+59=89	59

Lord Buddha in the preaching of the Abhidhamma described first the moral states as in "කුසලා ධම්මා අකුසලා ධම්මා අව්‍යාකතා ධම්මා" (Kusalādhammā, Akusalādhammā Aviyākatā dhammā) but The Venerable Anuruddha Mahā Thera who wrote the Abhidhamma Attha Sangaha described akusala or immoral states first in order that the subject matter might be more easily comprehended by the novice.

(1) Consciousness as experienced in Kāmalōka. Of these four what is consciousness as experienced in Kāmalōka?

TYPES OF IMMORAL CONSCIOUSNESS

(*a*) Types of Immoral Consciousness. These are eight classes of consciousness rooted in appetite or accompanied by greed or lust *viz*:—

1. Automatic consciousness accompanied by joy[2] and connected with error[3].

2. Volitional[1] consciousness accompanied by joy[2] and connected with error[3].

3. Automatic consciousness accompanied by joy[2] and disconnected from error[3].

4. Volitional[1] consciousness accompanied by joy and disconnected from error.

5. Automatic consciousness accompanied by indifference[4] and connected with error[3].

6. Volitional[1] consciousness accompanied by indifference[4] and connected with error[3].

7. Automatic consciousness accompanied by indifference[4] and disconnected from error[3].

8. Volitional[1] consciousness accompanied by indifference and disconnected from error[3].

NOTE 1.

In Dhamma Sangini classes of consciousness 2, 4, 6 & 8, are explicitly distinguished as sasankhārēna (සසංඛාරේන) as they are determined by another person or after some deliberation.

2. Sōmanassa (සොමනස්ස) here is ofpsycho logical import, meaning simply pleasurable feeling.

3. Diṭṭhi (දිට්ඨි) is erroneous opinion Micchā Diṭṭhi (මිච්ඡා දිට්ඨි) is here implied.

4. Upēkkhā (උපෙක්ඛා) here implies simply absence of felt pleasure or pain. It should be distinguished from the more complex intellectual and ethical upēkkhā (උපෙක්ඛා). *viz*:—Tatramajjhattatā (තත්‍රමජ්ඣත්තතා) balance of mind, equanimity.

Next, there are two classes of consciousness rooted in aversion, repugnance, or hate *viz* :—

9. Automatic consciousness accompanied by grief[1] and connected with aversion.[2]

10. Volitional consciousness accompanied by grief and connected with aversion.

Next there are two classes of consciousness rooted in nescience[3] *viz* :—

11. Consciousness accompanied by indifference and conjoined with perplexity.[4]

12. Consciousness accompanied by indifference and conjoined with distraction.[5]

NOTE 1.

1. Dōmanassa Sahagata (දොමනස්ස සහගත) is accompanied by grief. Grief is a state of mind present in the aggregate of feeling whose characteristic feature is to encounter unpleasant objects.

2. Paṭigha sampayutta (පටිඝ සම්පයුත්ත) is connected with aversion. Aversion is a mental property in the aggregate of sankhāras whose characteristic feature is, instead of being attached to objects, is to manifest repugnance to the object. Both grief and aversion always occur together, and never separately.

3. Mōmūha Cittāni (මොමූහචිත්තානි) confused or muddled consciousness. Mōha (මොහ) is used as a synonym of Avijjā (අවිජ්ජා) ignorance. Mōmūha (මොමූහ) is derived from the intensive form of the verb muyhati (මුය්හති) to be stupefied.

The reduplication, as in the case of 'dēvadēvō': (දෙවදෙවො) indicates that Mōha (මොහ) in these two classes, acts with greater force than the Mōha (මොහ) present in the foregoing ten classes of consciousness.

4. Vicikicchā (විචිකිච්ඡා) is doubt in respect of the Buddha, Dhamma, Sangha, The Precepts, the beginning, the end, both the beginning and the end, and dependent origination. There are also 16 types of doubt which will be detailed in the chapter on vipassanā (විපස්සනා).

5. Uddhacca (උද්ධච්ච) restlessness, the opposite of concentration rendered also by flurry and excitement. This mental property (though common to all classes of immoral thoughts) exists in an intensified form in this class of consciousness.

These summed up amount in all to twelve classes of immoral consciousness.

Aṭṭhadhā lōbha mūlāni dōsa mūlāni caddvidhā
Mōha mūlāni caddvēti dvādasākusalā siun

අට්ඨධා ලොභමූලානි දොසමූලානි චද්විධා
මොහමූලානි චද්වෙති ද්වාදසාකුසලාසියුං

Eight kinds of consciousness rooted in greed, two in aversion, and two in nescience make up the twelve classes of Immoral consciousness.

CAUSES OF JOY AND INDIFFERENCE

There are three roots or radical conditions necessary for the origination of joy or pleasurable interest *viz* (1) rebirth consciousness being one of the four classes accompanied by joy (2) object being pleasant (3) knowledge being not too deep and not possessed of insight. For being indifferent or having a neutral feeling too, there are three causes *viz* (1) rebirth consciousness by one of the six classes accompanied by indifference (2) object being neutal, neither pleasant nor unpleasant (3) possession of deep knowledge and keen insight.

CAUSES OF ERROR.

Two causes are responsible for the origination of error *viz* (1) erroneous ideas, perceptions and views regarding the three salient marks of transciency, sorrow and absence of a substantial entity. Thus falling into the two categories sāswata (ශාශ්වත), or ucchēda (උච්ඡේද) diṭṭhi (දිට්ඨි), that is belief in an everlasting entity or soul or atman or nothing after death. (2) association with people possessing such erroneous ideas, perceptions, and views. Immoral consciousness accompanied by error arises from the presence of these two causes, and that disconnected from error from their absence.

CAUSES OF AUTOMATIC CONSCIOUSNESS.

There are five causes assigned for the origination of automatic consciousness *viz* (1) suitable physical conditions (2) suitable residence (3) suitable food, (4) suitable clothing (5) and suitable associates. If any one or more of these are absent then volitional consciousness arises.

HOW CLASSES (1) AND (2) ARISE.

When a pleasant object in the possession of another individual is seen, consciousness is accompanied by joy. Thereafter he thinks of stealing that object contending that it is neither wrong nor improper for him to do so, as in a previous birth that individual had stolen some of his belongings and it is only the recovery of a debt. When the consciousness is accompanied by such erroneous views and ideas, then immoral consciousness accompanied by joy and connected with error arises with seven apperceptions (ජවන) Javana. It is automatic when not determined by another and volitional when determined by another or the act performed after some deliberation.

HOW CLASSES (3) AND (4) (5) (6) (7) (8) ARISE

Having seen an object in another's possession, if one were to steal same from greed and with joy, then an immoral consciousness arises. Though such be the case, if one contends that another is very wealthy and has many belongings and that it is not possible to maintain himself and his family without stealing, and he does so without being determined by another, then immoral automatic consciousness accompanied by joy and disconnected from error arises. When the act is performed, having been determined by another then it becomes volitional. In these four instances, when the object is not pleasant, the feeling is neutral or indifferent, and when determined by another it is volitional.

HOW CLASSES (9) AND (10) ARISE.

In the same manner classes of consciousness accompanied by grief and rooted in aversion can be understood. These classes are occasioned by two causes *viz* (1) an object that one dislikes (2) coming in contact with any of the nine types of actions that make a person angry, of which three are personal, three concerning a friend, and three an enemy. That this person scolded and abused me in a previous existence, and he does so now, and would do so in future ; concerning my friend too he acted similarly in the past, does so now, and would do so in the future; that he praised and helped my enemy in the past, does so now, and would do so in the future. In these nine ways a person may be made angry.

NUMBER OF STATES OF CONSCIOUSNESS INCALCULABLE.

These two classes of consciousness rooted in aversion or hate are present in killing, using abusive language and in hate and therefore should be reckoned as three. The amount so obtained should be multiplied by three according to the three periods of past, present and future. As the amount so obtained is present in one's person and in another, it should be multiplied by two. Next that amount should be multiplied by six according to their presence in the six doors such as eye etc. And that amount should be multiplied by two in respect of the city and country. Among the number of states of consciousness thus reckoned the number that arises in one individual in the round of births which has no beginning cannot even be compared to the amount obtained by measuring the four oceans with a mustard seed, or the earth with such space as would occupy a mustard seed. Therefore it will be seen that the number of such classes of consciousness rooted in aversion are incalculable and inestimable.

THE DOORS CAUSING THE THREE TYPES.

Of these 12 classes, 10 classes rooted in lust and aversion are obtained in Kamma by body and speech and cause the ten Akusala (අකුසල) Kamma. The two rooted in nescience are not obtained in Kamma by body and speech and appear only through the mind door.

CHAPTER II

CONSCIOUSNESS WITHOUT HĒTUS[1].

(*b*) Consciousness without Hētus[1]. There are seven classes of consciousness which are the results of evil done in a former birth to wit :—

(1) Consciousness by way of sight[2], accompanied by indifference.

(2)-(4) Consciousness by way of hearing, smell and taste, similarly accompanied.

(5) Consciousness by way of touch accompanied by pain[3].

(6) Recipient Consciousness accompanied by indifference.

(7) Investigating consciousness accompanied by indifference.

NOTE 1.

Ahētukāni cittāni (අහෙතුකානි චිත්තානි) unconditioned by one or more of the six radical conditions hētus (හෙතු) *viz*, greed, hate and ignorance, and their opposites disinterestedness, amity, and insight. In these seven classes of consciousness only the first three are responsible for the improper conduct in a former birth, the result whereof is now consciously experienced.

NOTES 2.

Consciousness by way of sight is cakkhu viññāna (චක්ඛු විඤ්ඤාණ). Here the eye (cakkhu චක්ඛු) is the sensitive material quality present in the ordinary eye or that quality present in the eye, which has originated from Kamma, as in previous births there was the craving to see visual objects, which is capable of cognizing objects. When the sensitive material quality in the eye comes in contact with a visual object through the help of light and attention of mind (මනසිකාර manasikāra) then consciousness by way of sight accompanied, by indifference (Upēkkhā sahagata cakkhu viññāna උපෙක්ඛා සහගත චක්ඛු විඤ්ඤාණ) arises. If the object happens to be an unpleasant one then theconsciousness is the result of evil done. Here the colour only of the visual object coming in contact with the sensitive material quality of the eye causes only a feeling of indifference and not joy or grief, like unto a piece of cotton coming in contact with another piece of cotton. Therefore that consciousness is called cognition of the eye accompanied by indifference and resulting from evil done in previous births. (akusala vipāka upekkhā sahagata cakkhuviññāna අකුසල විපාක උපෙක්ඛා සහගත චක්ඛු විඤ්ඤාණ). Similarly in respect of ear, nose and tongue.

NOTES 3.

But in respect of the body, the tactile consciousness is accompanied by pain (Dukkha sahagata Kāya viññāna දුක්ඛ සහගත කාය විඤ්ඤාණ). The reason for being so is explained thus :—Contact consists of the three great essentials, element of extension (පඨවි paṭhavi) element of heat (Tējō තෙජො) and element of motion (Vāyō වායො). When contact takes place the three elements mentioned above penetrates the sensitive element of the skin and comes in contact with the four great essentials in the body and the impression of the contact is very great. It is illustrated by the way in which a hammer comes in contact with another object penetrating a piece of cotton placed on same when a blow is given to the piece of cotton. When a pleasant object comes in contact with the body then the consciousness by way of touch is accompanied by joy.

Next there are eight[1] classes of consciousness which are the results of good done in a former birth and are without Hētus to wit :—

(8) Consciousness by way of sight accompanied by indifference.

(9)-(11) Consciousness by way of hearing smell and taste similarly accompanied.

(12) Consciousness by way of touch accompanied by joy.
(13) Recipient consciousness accompanied by indifference.
(14) Investigating consciousness accompanied by joy.
(15) Investigating consciousness accompanied by indifference.

Note 1.

CONSCIOUSNESS RESULTING FROM GOOD DONE IN FORMER BIRTHS.

When a pleasant object comes in contact with the sensitive material quality of the eye or a pleasant object is seen by the eye, cognition of the eye accompanied by indifference and resulting from good done in former births arises (Kusala vipāka upekkhā sahagata cakkhu viññāna කුසල විපාක උපෙක්ඛා සහගත චක්ඛු විඤ්ඤාණ). Similarly in respect of the ear, nose and tongue. When a pleasant touch comes in contact with the skin of the body, tactile cognition accompanied by joy and resulting from good done in previous births arises (Kusala vipāka sukha sahagata kāya viññāna කුසල විපාක සුඛ සහගත කාය විඤ්ඤාණ). Recipient consciousness accompanied by indifference is that whichreceives the pleasant object already perceived by the five senses (Kusala vipāka upēkkhā sahagata sampaṭicchana කුසල විපාක උපෙක්ඛා සහගත සම්පටිච්ඡන) The consciousness that investigates a very pleasant object is accompanied by joy (Kusala vipāka sōmanassa sahagata santīrana කුසල විපාක සොමනස්ස සහගත සන්තීරන and that which investigates a moderately pleasant object is accompanied by indifference (Kusala vipāka upēkkhā sahagata santīrana. කුසල විපාක උපෙක්ඛා සහගත සන්තීරන).

VARIATION OF FEELING ACCORDING TO INDIVIDUAL.

It must be understood that what is pleasant to one individual may be unpleasant to another and *vice versa.* For instance a pleasant object appears unpleasant to one who has erroneous perceptions and ideas such as the sight of the Buddha's image, and an unpleasant thing appears pleasant such as a carcase or excreta which is indulged in by some kinds of animals. Again what is pleasant to one " sense door " may be unpleasant to another " sense door ' for instance a sharp cutting instrument made of gold and silver though pleasant to the eye is unpleasant to the body. A speck of excreta or other dirt though not unpleasant to the eye is unpleasant to the nose. When a worldling sees urine excreta etc. at first cognition of the eye resulting from bad deeds done in a previous birth arises and therefore apperceptions (ජවන Javana) rooted in aversion arise. But when they are seen by a dog or a pig cognition of the eye resulting from good deeds alone in previous births arises and thereafter apperceptions rooted in lust and greed arise. If a worldling having seen such urine, excreta etc. contemplates that inside his body too there are impurities of this nature, then great moral classes of consciousness arise and the apperceptions are moral. Buddhas, Paccēka Buddhas, and Arahats after seeing such impurities develop great unmoral or ineffective apperceptions.

Next there are three classes of consciousness without Hētus (හෙතු) and ineffective[1] to wit :—

(16) Consciousness turning to impression at the five doors[2] accompanied by indifference.

(17) Consciousness turning to impression at the mind-door[3] similary accompanied.

(18) Consciousness of the genesis of aesthetic pleasure[4] accompanied by joy.

These summed up amount in all to eighteen classes of consciousness without Hētus (හෙතු).

NOTES 1.

Kriyā or Kiriya (ක්‍රියා or කිරිය) effecting no Karma (කර්‍ම).

NOTES 2.

Āvajjana (ආවජ්ජන) is derived from Avattēti to 'turn towards' and 'reflection' is its nearest etymological equivalent. This, however, is not adequate, for Pancadvārāvajjana (පඤ්චද්වාරාවජ්ජන) is never a phase of representative cognition nor is Manodvārāvajjana (මනො මාරාවජ්ජන) confined to purely representative cognition. Anger is felt directly as a mental presentation. Hence the phrase 'turning tọ' has been adopted to cover all cases. At this stage the object is not yet perceived.

TURNING TO IMPRESSIONS AT THE FIVE DOORS.

When no object comes within the avenue of the sense doors, consciousness or mind is still and motionless as in deep sleep and is called the life continnum (bhavanga භවංග). The life continnum may be compared to a spider resting motionless and still in the middle of the web. When any object comes within the avenue of one of the five doors of sense then the life continnum is first disturbed and later arrested and then turns to or directs its attention to find out through what door the object came. This is called turning to impressions at the five doors (pancadvārāvajjana පංචවාරාවජ්ජන). It is likened to the spider who is disturbed by an insect resting in one of the threads of the web and also turns to or directs its attention to find out in which thread the insect is resting. It is too feeble to cause joy or grief and therefore it is accompanied by indifference. It is not the result of good or bad kamma in previous births, and likewise as it does not produce any results it is neither good nor bad kammá. It is solely ineffective.

NOTES 3.

MANODVĀRĀ VAJJANA MIND DOOR CONSCIOUSNESS.

The consciousness that turns to impressions at the mind door is also accompanied by indifference and is called upēkkhā sahagata manodvārāvajjana (උපෙක්ඛා සහගත මනොවාරාවජ්ජන.) Mind-door is the life continuum that turns to impressions. In process of thought through the five doors it is called determining consciousness (votthapana citta වොත්ථපන චිත්ත). This too is neither a Kamma nor a result, and it is solely ineffective.

NOTES 4.

GENESIS OF AESTHETIC PLEASURE.

Consciousness of the genesis of aesthetic pleasure accompanied by joy is somanassa sahagata hasituppāda (සොමනස්ස සහගත හසිතුප්පාද). This is confined to the Paccēka Buddha and Arahats only and it is an ineffective class of consciousness that make them laugh on receiving impressions through any of the doors.

LAUGHTER.

There are thirteen classes of consciousness which cause laughter *viz.* (1) Four classes of immoral consciousness accompanied by joy and rooted in lust or greed (2) Four classes of great moral consciousness accompanied by joy (3) four classes of great ineffective consciousness accompanied by joy and (4) This one of the genesis of aesthetic pleasure accompanied by joy. Of these No. (1) and (2), that is eight in all, cause laughter in the worldlings (puthujjanas පුථුජ්ජන). In sēkha puggala සේඛ පුග්ගල) those who have entered the first three Paths, and the accompanied Fruits, laughter is caused by the two classes of immoral consciousness disconnected from error and accompanied by joy and the four great moral classes accompanied by joy. In Arahats and Paccēka Buddhas the four great inoperative classes accompanied by joy, and this one of the genesis of aesthetic pleasure accompanied by joy cause laughter Only two classes of consciousness, to wit, the two great inoperative classes accompanied by joy and connected with insight cause laughter in the Buddhas. With the exception of the ineffective class of consciousness of the genesis of aesthetic pleasure accompanied by joy, the other twelve not only cause laughter but also perform other functions. How is laughter caused in Arahats through the five doors of sense? When a residence or a seat suitable for practising insight (විපස්සනා vipassana) with supreme effort is seen by the eye then laughter is caused through the 'eye-door'.

When the Puthujjana (පුථුජ්ජන) Bhikkhus make a tremendous noise like fishmongers at the place of distribution of various articles amongst themselves laughter is caused through the 'ear-door' reflecting that the Arahat has completely extinguished the āsavās and that he has no clinging for such articles. When a sweet smell emanating from camphor, sweet smelling flowers etc. come in contact with the sensitive material quality of the nose, the Arahat thinks that this smell is suitable to be offered to the Buddha and laughter is caused through the 'nose-door'. When an Arahat obtains by begging alms a bowl of food of extremely good taste and shares it with the other Brothers then laughter is caused through the 'tongue-door'. When the Brothers personally attend to the bodily comforts of the Arahats such as massaging the limbs etc. then laughter is caused through the 'body-door'.

Laughter is of six kinds to, wit (1) Sita (සිත), (2) Hasita (හසිත), (3) Vihasita (විහසිත), (4)Up ahasita (උපහසිත), (5) Apahasita (අපහසිත), and (6) Atihasita (අතිහසිත). Of these sita (සිත) is manifestation of pleasurable interest by the face and ear. Only this type of laughter originates in a Buddha (2) Hasita (හසිත) is laughter exposing teeth (3) Vihasita (විහසිත) is laughter with a pleasant noise. (4) Upahasita (උපහසිත) is laughter with shrugging of shoulders (5) Apahasita (අපහසිත) is laughter with full of tears, and (6) Atihasita (අතිහසිත) is laughter with the inclining of the body forwards and backwards.

Sattākusala pākāni puññapākāni aṭṭhadhā
Kriyā cittāni tīnīti aṭṭhārasa ahētukā

සත්තා කුසල පාකානි පුඤ්ඤපාකානි අට්ඨධා
ක්‍රියා චිත්තානි තීණීති අට්ඨාරස අහේතුකා

Seven kinds of consciousness from past wrong deeds, eight from past meritorious deeds and three bringing no result make up in all eighteen classes without Hētus (හේතු).

Pāpāhētuka muttāni sōbhanānīti vuccarē
Ekūnasaṭṭhi cittāni Athēkanavuthīpivā

පාපාහේතුක මුත්තානි සෝභනානීති වුච්චරේ
එකූනසට්ඨි චිත්තානි අථේකනවුතීපිවා

Excluding the immoral thoughts and those without hētus (හේතු) there are fifty nine or ninety one classes of consciousness called beautiful.

CHAPTER III

THE GREAT[1] TYPES OF MORAL CONSCIOUSNESS

There are eight classes of consciousness of a moral kind arising in Kāmalōka experience to wit :—

1 Automatic[4] consciousness accompanied by joy[3] and connected with knowledge[2] .

2 Volitional consciousness accompanied by joy and connected with knowledge.

3 Automatic consciousness accompanied by joy and disconnected from knowledge.

4 Volitional consciousness accompanied by joy and disconnected from knowledge.

5 Automatic consciousness accompanied by indifference and connected with knowledge.

6 Volitional consciousness accompanied by indifference and connected with knowledge.

7 Automatic consciousness accompanied by indifference and disconnected from knowledge.

8 Volitional consciousness accompanied by indifference and disconnected from knowledge.

NOTE 1

1 The word Mahā (මහා) is usually prefixed to higher classes of Kāmalōka, consciousness to indicate a more extensive field of action.

2 N̄ana sampayuttañ (ඤාණසම්පයුත්තං). Into this class of consciousness the cētasika (චේතසික), the mental property called faculty of reason, (පඤ්ඤින්ද්‍රිය paññindriya) enters, giving the class its specific character (ඤාණ) (ñana) and (පඤ්ඤින්ද්‍රිය) (paññindriya) are used as interchangeable terms.

CAUSES OF JOY IN MORAL CONSCIOUSNESS

3 Nine factors are deemed to be necessary for the origination of joy in the great types of moral consciousness *viz* (1) possession of suitable articles for offering, (2) presence of a suitable person fit to receive offerings (3) presence of a suitable period (4) presence of a suitable place where Buddhism prevails (5) presence of good associates (6) possession of right views (7) a knowledge of the virtues of the person who is to receive the offerings (8) a belief in the good resultant effects that would accrue by charity, and (9) rebirth consciousness being one of the four accompanied by joy. If one or more of these are absent, classes of consciousness accompanied by indifference arise.

CAUSES OF KNOWLEDGE IN MORAL CONSCIOUSNESS

Five factors are deemed to be necessary for the origination of knowledge in the great types of moral consciousness *viz*:—

1 Teaching of the Dhamma vinaya, arts and sciences in a previous birth and hoping to derive knowledge thereby (2) the offering of oil lamps and other articles such as would be profitable and useful to those who preach the doctrine or to students who learn, the Dhamma hoping to derive knowledge thereby in subsequent existences.

(3) The study of mathematics, science, art, writing of books on profitable and useful subjects architecture and so on. (4) reaching the decade in which the faculty of reason is at its acme and (5) at the moment of giving charity the moral consciousness should be free from greed, hate, and delusion. If all these five factors are accompanied then the greatest moral consciousness arises, which is capable of causing a Tihētuka Paṭisandhi (තිහෙතුක පටිසන්ධි) that is rebirth consciousness associated with disinterestedness, amity and knowledge, and indispensable and absolutely necessary rebirth consciousness for developing the Jhānas and for entering the Paths.

If one or more of the above are not present, the class of consciousnesses that arises is one disconnected from knowledge.

AUTOMATIC MORAL CONSCIOUSNESS

Note 4.

There are six causes responsible for this great type of moral consciousness to be automatic, namely (1) being absolutely free from selfishness and placing the article of offering in the hands of the person who receives the same and (2) the firm belief in the fact that as a result of this charity, good effects will undoubtedly take place according to the nature of the offering (3) suitable residence (4) suitable environment (5) suitable food and (6) being accustomed to give charity. If one or more of these causes are absent, the class of consciousness will be volitional.

FACTORS CAUSING DIFFERENT CLASSES.

In the first one of the eight classes of the great moral consciousness 38 mental concomitants such as contact (phassa ඵස්ස) are coexistent. Each class is associated with feeling (vēdanā වේදනා) and knowledge (ñāna ඤාණ) automatic or volitional. Feeling is differentiated into joy or pleasurable feeling and indifferent or neutral feeling. Knowledge is differentiated into insight (vipassanā විපස්සනා), in which case ñāna sampayuttañ is the existence of the paññā cētasika (පඤ්ඤාචේතසික) and ordinary knowledge without insight, which is ñānavippayuttan, paññā cētasika (පඤ්ඤාචේතසික) being absent here. How ordinary knowledge exists in both classes can be explained by the following illustration :—

වස්සකාතො සුභික්ඛො දුබ්භික්ඛො (vassakatō subhikkhō dubbhikkō). Harvest or famine results through rain, both the states being connected with rain. Likewise, when there is insight or no insight both the classes are connected with knowledge.

Sankhāra (සඞ්ඛාර) should not be considered as a mental concomitant coexistent in consciousness Sankhāra (සඞ්ඛාර) is the preparation for the origination of a state of consciousness determined either by another individual or by an antecedent state of consciousness in one's self.

AUTOMATIC AND VOLITIONAL CONSCIOUSNESS

People who have got into the habit of doing good Kamma themselves think and automatically practice charity. Those who have a greed for their possessions and are selfish and are not naturally generous practise after some deliberation and after receiving advice from others. Therefore, the manner in which automatic (asankhāra අසංඛාර) and volitional (sasankhāra සසංඛාර) classes of consciousness originate can be compared to the cutting by a sharp instrument, and a blunt instrument that is sharpened. This great moral consciousness arising in Kāmalōka may not produce results in a process of thought through the 'five doors' such as 'eye-door' etc. as well as the 'mind-door' or produce results in a 'mind-door' process. Out of these the great moral consciousness arising in a process, of thought through the 'five-doors' and not producing results can be compared to the fragrance and sweet smell emanating from a tree full of fruits, that through the 'mind-door' to unripe and unseasoned fruits falling from the tree and that which produce results in a 'mind-door' process to a ripe and well seasoned fruit having colour, smell, and taste. Similarly, as a result of a moral consciousness arising in a process of thought through the 'five-doors' by the mere sight, hearing, smell, taste, and contact of others, the results of good unconditioned by hētus (හේතු) are obtained during existence. The result of a moral consciousness arising in a process of thought through the 'mind-door' and not producing results is the unhappy existence obtained by labour etc. and working hard for others without adequate wages. Lastly, the result of great moral consciousness arising in 'mind-door' process producing results when intensified is the rebirth in the six heavens as great dēvas, and in the world of men as Chakkawatti king and other high positions according to the Kamma done, and as a matter of fact obtaining anything hoped for at the time of the act. In cases of consciousness less intensified but belong to great and moral classes happiness is obtained by such efforts as doing agricultural work, trade etc.

9—16[1] next there are eight classes of consciousness, similar to the foregoing which are the results of action done in a former birth in Kāmalōka, and which are accompanied by their hētus (හේතු).

CLASSES OF RESULTANT CONSCIOUSNESS

NOTE 1

These resultant classes of consciousness are similar to the moral classes like the shadow of an object being more or less similar to the object that produces it.

These classes exist in an individual as rebirth consciousness, life continuum, retention and re-decease. When they exist as rebirth consciousness they are called rebirth resultants (paṭisandhi vipāka පටිසන්ධි විපාක). When they exist as life-continuum, retention and re-decease they are known as resultants during the span of life or existence (pavatti vipāka පවත්ති විපාක). Rebirth is conception in a new existence or the joining together of two existences. Life continuum (භවංග Bhavanga) is consciousness lying still and motionless without taking any impressions through the doors of eye etc. Retention is the ability to retain such objects as have been grasped by apperceptions (Javana ජවන) in processes of thought. Re-decease is the passing away from an existence.

FACTORS ASSOCIATED WITH THE CLASSES AND THEIR CAUSES

The first four classes are accompanied by joy and the cause for it is the obtaining of pleasant objects and the other four are accompanied by indifference and the cause for it, the obtaining of a moderately pleasant object.

Of these, first and second, fifth and sixth classes are connected with knowledge. There are two causes for making them so. When they exist as rebirth consciousness, life continuum and re-decease, owing to the intensity of the Kamma which produced them they become connected with knowledge.

Rebirth caused by the highest class of moral consciousness associated with the three hētus (හෙතු). (Tihētuka mukkatthan kusalan kamman තිහෙතුක මුක්කට්ඨං කුසලං කම්මං), become connected with knowledge amounting to insight. As the life continuum and re-decease are similar to the rebirth consciousness in that existence, the intensity of this kamma is the cause of making the life continuum and re-decease connected with knowledge. The other cause is when they exist as retention they become connected with knowledge following the apperceptions which are connected with knowledge.

The three hētus (හේතු) are disinterestedness, amity, and insight and the moral consciousness becomes the highest when the preceding and following series are also associated with the three hētus (හේතු).

Similarly the third and fourth, the seventh and eighth classes are disconnected from knowledge. The two causes for doing so are the weakness of the Kamma and retaining the objects grasped by the apperceptions disconnected from knowledge. When they exist as rebirth, life continuum and re-decease, they are disconnected from knowledge by reason of the weakness of the Kamma performed previously. Rebirth, life continuum and re-decease occasioned by a Kamma which is associated with the three hētus (හේතු) but not of the highest class and that of two hētus (හේතු) of the highest class and disconnected from knowledge. When they exist as retention, retaining the object grasped by the apperceptions disconnected from knowledge, they become themselves disconnected from knowledge. The first, the third, fifth and seventh classes are automatic. They become so when the Kamma, the sign of Kamma (Kamma කම්ම nimitta නිමිත්ත) and the sign of destiny (gati nimitta ගති නිමිත්ත) are not determined by another individual and also when suitable physical conditions, food etc. could be secured.

The second, fourth, sixth and eighth are volitional. They become so when the Kamma, the sign of Kamma and the sign of destiny are determined by another individual and the absence of suitable physical conditions food etc.

17—24,[1] next there are eight classes of consciousness arising in Kāmalōka, which are accompanied by their hētus (හේතු) but are ineffective. These again are similar to the first eight. These summed up amount in all to twenty four classes of consciousness of moral, resultant, and ineffective kinds which arise in Kāmalōka and are accompanied by their hētus (හේතු).

INEFFECTIVE CLASSES OF CONSCIOUSNESS

NOTE 1

These eight classes originate only in Arahats, in whom there is the extinction of āsavās. These are not moral classes as they do not produce any resultants but are ineffective.

Vēdanāñāna sankhāra bhēdēna catuveesati
Sahētukāmāvacara puññapāka kriyā matā

වෙදනා ඤාණ සඞ්ඛාර භෙදෙන චතුවීසති
සහෙතුකාමාවචර පුඤ්ඤපාක ක්‍රියා මතා

In Kamaloka consciousness we see three classes together with their hētus [1]. First there is one which brings merit and then one brought by previous merit and then again a class whereupon results can never be. Divide these three according as they show feeling, knowledge, and volition. Now eight modes appear in each. Thus there are 24 classes associated with their hētus (හෙතු).

NOTE 1

Of these, the twelve classes unconnected with knowledge, that is in the 24 classes mentioned above, Nos. 2, 4, 6, 8, 10, 12, 14, 16, and so on are said to be accompanied by two of the hētus (හෙතු) *viz.* disinterestedness (alōbha අලොභ) and love or amity (adōsa අදොස). The corresponding twelve connected with knowledge that is No. 1, 3, 5, 7, 9, 11, and so on are said to be accompanied by three hētus (හෙතු) *viz.* the two above mentioned and knowledge or intelligence (amōha අමොහ).

2 Sankhāra (සඞ්ඛාර) that is pubba abhisankhāro (පුබ්බ අභිසඞ්ඛාරො) or previous volitional effort on the part of self or another.

(Summary of Kāmalōka Consciousness)

Kāmētēveesapākāni puññapuññāni veesati
Ēkādasa kriyā cēti catupaññāsa sabbathā

කාමෙතෙවීසපාකානි පුඤ්ඤාපුඤ්ඤානි වීසති
එකාදස ක්‍රියා චෙති චතුපඤ්ඤාස සබ්බථා

Twenty three kinds of resultants. Twenty kinds of good and bad Kamma, and eleven kinds of unmoral or ineffective, which bring the total to 54.

CHAPTER IV.

2. CONSCIOUSNESS AS EXPERIENCED IN RŪPALŌKA

MORAL CONSCIOUSNESS.

There are five classes of consciousness which in Rūpalōka are moral and arise as Rūpa mind to wit :—

1. Moral consciousness of the 1st stage of Jhāna[1]. This occurs with initial application, sustained application[2], pleasurable interest[3], pleasure[4] and one pointedness[5].

2. Moral consciousness of the 2nd stage of Jhāna. This occurs together with sustained application, pleasurable interest, pleasure, and one pointedness.

3. Moral consciousness of the 3rd stage of Jhāna. This occurs together with pleasurable interest, pleasure, and one pointedness.

4. Moral consciousness of the 4th stage of Jhāṇa. This occurs together with pleasure and one pointedness.

5. Moral consciousness of the 5th stage of Jhāna. This occurs together with hedonic indifference and one pointedness.

Next, there are five classes of Rūpalōka consciousness, which are the results of Jhānas, to wit :—

6—10 Resultant[6] consciousness of each of the five stages of Jhāna characterized as above.

Next, there are five classes of Rūpalōka consciousness which are ineffective to wit :—

11—15 Ineffective consciousness of each of the five stages of Jhāna characterized as above.

NOTE 1

Rapt systematized meditation, getting into the state of ecstasy is the meaning of the term Jhāna. A state of consciousness cannot arise free from the mental concomitants. Of the 35 mental concomitants such as contact, feeling and so on coexisting in moral consciousness of Rūpalōka, only five are particularly manifested as only they arise in Jhāna. Just as when the different parts such as the engine, chassis, hood, body, and wheels in a motor car are all combined it is called a motor car, so the group of mental concomitants initial application (විතක්කො vitakko) sustained application (විචාරො vicāro) pleasurable interest (පීති pīti) pleasure (සුඛ sukha) and one pointedness (ඒකග්ගතා ēkaggatā) is called Jhāna. It is also called Jhāna because it applies itself on an object and also because it inhibits such Torments as the five Hindrances. Initial application causes consciousness to apply itself on an object. Sustained application causes consciousness to apply itself on the object continuously and in a sustained manner. Pleasurable interest causes consciousness to derive pleasurable interest from the object. Pleasure causes consciousness to partake of the taste of the object. One pointedness causes consciousness to be concentrated or one-pointed without being distracted.

Initial application inhibits sloth and torpor; sustained application inhibits doubt; pleasurable interest inhibits hate; pleasure inhibits restlessness and worry; one pointedness inhibits sense desires. In this manner when consciousness is accompanied by these five properties, it is called moral consciousness of the 1st stage of Jhāna.

HOW JHANA CAN BE DEVELOPED.

The way in which the 1st stage of Jhāna could be developed will be briefly stated here.

The individual whose rebirth consciousness is associated with the three hētus (හෙතු) and who is determined to practice mental culture (Tihētuka yogāwacarayā තිහෙතුක යොගාවචරයා) having considered the futility of the so-called happiness, which is only transient, that could be desired by gratifying the senses both in the world of men and in the worlds of Devas, desires to obtain happiness from concentration (samādhi- සමාධි) or one-pointedness in this world, and happiness of the Brahmas in future existences. Out of the 40 stations of exercise in calm such as the hypnotic circle of earth and so on, he obtains a station of exercise suitable to his character, observes the five, eight, or the ten precepts with Tisarana and gets into a place of solitude which is free from the ten palibōdhas (පලිබොධ) which would retard one's progress in mental culture and then he practises exercises in mental culture or concentration. In the event of his selecting the hypnotic circle of earth (පඨවි කසිණ), he makes the circle of earth a span and four inches in diameter with dawn colour clay as described in detail in such works as Visuddhi-magga and Path of Purity, places it before him, gazing at it repeats " (පඨවි පඨවි) as many times as possible. It may be hundreds or thousands. The hypnotic circle of earth is called the preliminary symbol (parikamma nimitta පරිකම්ම නිමිත්ත). When this exercise is practised for some time the preliminary symbol is not grasped by the eye but by the mind. Whether he closes his eye or looks at another direction a symbol similar to the preliminary symbol appears at the mind-door as if he saw it with the eye. This symbol is called the symbol of the image and culture becomes well established. Later on, in the case of one who is thus well established, and who, after that advanced stage, gives himself to sustained contemplation concerning the symbol of the image, with the degree of concentration gained from the preliminary stage, then, when that object similar to the image symbol freed from its physical base, reckoned as a concept, and accomplished by culture-practice is well established in and well driven into the mind, the transformed after-image is said to have been well developed. The transformed after-image is called the paṭibhāga nimitta (පටිභාග නිමිත්ත). It appears as a brilliant light in various shapes according to individuals, as if a light came through the moon. Coming through the symbol of the image this culture is called the accessory stage of mental culture (upacāra bhāvana උපචාර භාවනා). Thenceforth contemplation by way of the accessory stage, stripped of obstacles and called concentration of Kāmalōka experience is said to be accomplished. After that, to one who has maintained that transformed after-image by accessory concentration the 1st Jhāna of the Rūpalōka supervenes.

FIVE HABITS.

After that, to one who has cultivated the 1st Jhāna by means of the five habits, to wit (1) turning the attention to the 1st Jhāna (āvajjana vasitā ආවජ්ජන වසිතා) (2) inducing and maintaining it (samāpajjana vasitā සමාපජ්ජන වසිතා) (3) pre-determining the period of its maintenance (adhiṭṭhāna vasitā අධිට්ඨාන වසිතා) (4) emerging from it (vuṭṭhāna vasitā වුට්ඨාන වසිතා) and (5) reflecting on it (pacca vekkhana vasitā පච්චවෙක්ඛන වසිතා) for the purpose of putting away the grosser features beginning with the initial imagination and so on, and of striving to bring about the subtler features, beginning with sustained imagination etc., the 2nd and higher Jhānas supervene in one order.

2 Sustained application is vitakka (විතක්ක) and vicāra (විචාර).

3 Pleasurable interest is Pīti (පීති) whereby aversion is inhibited byāpada (බ්‍යාපාද). It creates an interest in the object, at first a dull or slight sense of interest (khuddaka pīti ඛුද්දක පීති) growing keener and keener through oscillating interest (okkantika pīti ඔක්කන්තික පීති) into an intense interest amounting to thrilling emotion (ubbēga pīti උබ්බේග පීති) followed finally by interest amounting to rapture (pharana pīti ඵරන පීති). This diffused rapture is invariably followed by pleasurable easeful, happy feeling (sukha සුඛ) by which distraction and worry (uddhacca kukkucca උද්ධච්ච කුක්කුච්ච) are inhibited.

4 The psychological, and not the ethical pleasure (sukha සුඛ) cētasika vedanā (චේතසික වේදනා).

5 One-pointedness is ēkaggatā (ඒකග්ගතා). This is the element, the consciousness, of awareness of one object and one only, because, by the selective act, the mind is not distracted by several different objects. Literally 'one pointedness' as to object of attention.

6 Resultant consciousness is that consciousness caused by the effect of Jhāna practised in the immediate preceding life.

RESULTANT CONSCIOUSNESS.

The five classes of resultant consciousness are similar to the five classes of moral consciousness in Rūpalōka. It is compared to the image seen through a looking-glass resembling the person.

REBIRTH IN REALMS OF BRAHMA LOKA.

Those who have developed the five classes of moral consciousness in respect of the five stages of Jhāna obtain rebirth consciousness, life continuum and re-decease by the five classes of resultant consciousness. If one were to practise in this existence exercises in mental culture such as a hypnotic circle and obtain moral consciousness of the 1st stage of Jhāna in a slight degree and possesses the factors of the 1st Jhāna just before death, he will be reborn in the realm of Brahma's retinue (Brahma pārisajja බ්‍රහ්මපාරිසජ්ජ). The first consciousness arising there is rebirth consciousness (paṭisandhi citta පටිසන්ධිචිත්ත). From that time as long as he is in that existence without impressions being taken by any of the sense organs or the three doors such as eye-door, ear-door, and mind-door consciousness that arises is known as life continuum (bhavanga භවංග). The last consciousness in that existence is known as re-decease (චුතිචිත්ත cuti cītta). Rebirth consciousness, life continuum and re-decease, as they are the results of moral consciousness of the 1st stage of Jhāna developed in this existence are called resultant consciousness. They are possessed of the Jhāna factors, initial application, sustained application, pleasurable interest, pleasure and one pointedness and are known as the resultant consciousness of the 1st stage of Jhāna.

If the moral consciousness of the 1st stage of Jhāna is developed in a moderate degree then he will be reborn in the realm of Brahma's Ministers (Brahma Purōhita බ්‍රහ්ම පුරෝහිත) and when in a very great degree in the realm of Māha Brahma. These three are known as the planes of the 1st stage of Jhāna.

When the 2nd and 3rd stages of Jhāna are cultivated in a minor degree rebirth takes place in the heaven of minor lustre (parittābha පරිත්තාභ) in a moderate degree in the heaven of infinite lustre (Appamānābha අප්පමාණාභ) and in a very great degree in the heaven of the radiant gods (the gods from whose bodies the rays of light are emitted like lightning) (ābhassara ආභස්සර). This is the plane of 2nd Jhāna.

When the 4th stage of Jhāna is cultivated in a minor degree rebirth takes place in the heaven of the gods of minor aura (paritta subha පරිත්ත සුභ), in a moderate degree in the heaven of the Gods of infinite aura (Appamāna subha අප්පමාණ සුභ), and in a very great degree in the heaven of the gods full of steady aura (a mass of steady light emitted from the body) Subhakinha සුභකිණ්හ). This is the plane of 3rd Jhāna.

When the 5th stage of Jhāna is cultivated rebirth takes place in the realm of the gods of the great reward (වෙහප්ඵලං vehapphalan — විපුලංඵලං Vipulanphalan, that is, abundant reward, great compared with the reward of the lower Brahmas). The same cultivated in such a manner as to totally extirpate consciousness causes rebirth in the realm of the unconscious beings (asañña sattā අසඤ්ඤ සත්තා), and those who have become Never-Returners (Anāgāmi අනාගාමි) in the realm of the Pure Abodes (Suddhāvāsa සුද්ධාවාස). This is the plane of the 4th Jhāna. In all these planes resultant consciousness arising as rebirth, life continuum and re-decease should be understood in the same manner as was stated in connection with the resultant consciousness of the 1st Jhāna.

INEFFECTIVE CONSCIOUSNESS IN BRAHMA LŌKA

When an Arahat, in whom there is extinction of the āsavās, cultivates the 1st stage of Jhāna associated with the five factors of 1st stage of Jhāna in a moral consciousness, then that class is called ineffective. Similarly with the other Jhānas. They produce no results.

These, summed up, amount in all to fifteen classes of Rūpalōka consciousness, moral resultant and ineffective.

Pancadhā Jhānabhēdēna rūpāvacara mānasan
Puññapāka kriyā bhēdhātan pancadasadhā bhavē

පඤ්චධා ඣානභෙදෙන රූපාවචර මානසං
පුඤ්ඤපාක ක්‍රියා භෙධාතං පඤ්චදසධා භවෙ

" Five fold our thoughts on Rūpalōka's plane,
E'en as five fold of Jhāna is the chain,
As making merit, or as just effect,
Or bringing none gives fifteen as correct."

CHAPTER V

3. Consciousness as experienced in Arūpalōka[1].

Of Arūpa Jhāna.

CLASSES OF CONSCIOUSNESS AS EXPERIENCED IN ARŪPALŌKA.

There are four classes of consciousness which are moral and arise as Arūpa-mind, to wit :—

1. Moral consciousness dwelling on the infinity of space[2].

2. Moral consciousness dwelling on the infinity of consciousness.

3. Moral consciousness dwelling on Nothingness.

4. Moral consciousness wherein perception neither is nor is not[2].

Next there are four classes of consciousness, which are results of Jhānas by similar kinds practised in the life immediately previous, to wit :—

5—8[3] Resultant consciousness of each of the four objects of thought characterized as above.

Next, there are four classes of consciousness which bring no result and belong to Arūpalōka, to wit :—

9—12[4] Ineffective consciousness of each of the four objects of thought characterized as above.

These, summed up, amount in all to twelve classes of consciousness in Arūpalōka, moral, resultant and ineffective.

NOTE 1.

Dhammasangini 265-8.

NOTE 2.

According to the Tīkās, the citta (චිත්ත) has as its object the infinity of space; the second citta (චිත්ත) has as its object the first citta (චිත්ත) or viññāna (විඤ්ඤාණ); the third citta (චිත්ත) has as its object the first citta (චිත්ත) regarded as "nothing". The object of the 4th citta (චිත්ත) is consciousness of any Kind—Saññā (සඤ්ඤා) being a symbolical or representative term—wherein complete hypnosis is all but attained. Perception can therefore be taken in its older wider sense as 'that act whereby the mind becomes conscious of anything'. Buddhaghōsa, commenting on the term in The Mahā Niddana Suttanta, remarks neither viññāna (විඤ්ඤාණ) nor not viññāna (විඤ්ඤාණ) as well as neither saññā (සඤ්ඤා) etc. So subtle and delicate is the consciousness.

3. Dhammasangini 501.

4. Dhammasangini 579.

JHĀNA CONCERNED WITH THE ARŪPALŌKA.

To one who practises his preliminary exercise, by way of infinity, on space obtained by abstraction from any of the hypnotic circles except the space circle (because one cannot abstract space from space), the 1st stage of Arūpa Jhāna supervenes (ākāsānancāyatana Kusala cittan ආකාසානඤ්චායතන කුසල චිත්තං). The formula for repetition in this exercise is 'space is infinite', 'space is infinite', (anantō ākāsō anantō ākāsō, අනන්තො ආකාසො අනන්තො ආකාසො). How is this Jhāna developed? The individual who has developed the five stages of Rūpalōka Jhāna in the manner stated before, having realized the uselessness or futility of the physical body, as it is subject to all kinds of disease and because of its presence one quarrels enters into controversies and do such manner of things as may bring one great suffering, being desirous of completely eradicating the physical body, selects one of the nine hypnotic circles (Kasina කසිණ) excepting that of space for reason stated before, and develops the 4th stage of Jhāna in Rūpalōka. Thereafter he awakes from the 4th stage of Jhāna and diffuses the transformed after-image of the kasina (කසිණ) object in any locality to such a distance as pleases him. So long as he pays no attention to the diffused transformed after-image, he only sees space there. Then he obtains space by abstraction from the transformed after-image and continues to repeat the formula (anantō ākāsō anantō ākāsō අනන්තො ආකාසො අනන්තො ආකාසො). When practising so, for a considerable period, no sooner than the five hindrances are inhibited, there arises 1st Jhāna of Arūpalōka (ākāsānancāyatana Kusala cittan ආකාසානඤ්චායතන කුසල චිත්තං)

2ND JHĀNA.

To one who, by way of infinity, practices his preliminary exercise on the cognition of the 1st Arūpa stage, the 2nd stage of Arūpa-Jhāna supervenes (viññānancāyatana Kusala cittan විඤ්ඤාණඤ්චායතන කුසල චිත්තං). The formula for repetition in this exercise is 'consciousness is infinite, consciousness is infinite' (anantan viññānan anantan viññānan අනන්තං විඤ්ඤාණං අනන්තං විඤ්ඤාණං). Anantan viññānan or consciousness is infinite refers here to the consciousness of the 1st Arūpa Jhāna. How is the 2nd Jhāna developed? The individual who has developed the 1st stage of Arūpa Jhāna, just as a person who is frightened of a snake will get frightened on seeing any material resembling a snake, he gets disgusted of the 1st stage of Arūpa Jhāna developed from eradication of the physical body, and with the hope of eradicating same he makes the consciousness of the 1st stage of Jhāna his object and practises repeating the formula above stated. To one who so practises in course of time with the inhibition of the Five Hindrances there arises the 2nd stage of Arūpa Jhāna (viññānancāyatana Kusala cittan විඤ්ඤාණඤ්චායතන කුසල චිත්තං).

3RD JHĀNA.

To one who practises his preliminary exercise on the non-existence of the aforesaid cognition of the 1st Arūpa stage, mentally repeating 'there is naught whatever there is naught whatever.' (නත්ථි කිඤ්චි නත්ථි කිඤ්චි natthi kinci natthi kinci), the 3rd stage of Arūpa Jhāna supervenes. He who has developed the 1st stage of Jhāna, no sooner than he develops the 2nd stage, will realize that his consciousness of the 1st stage has disappeared. The disappearance itself is stated here 'as naught whatever'. The Jhāna consciousness which supervenes, having for its object 'there is naught whatever' or (natthi kinci නත්ථි කිඤ්චි) is called the 3rd stage of Arūpa Jhāna (ākincaññāyatana Kusala cittan ආකිඤ්චඤ්ඤායතන කුසල චිත්තං). How can the 3rd Jhāna be developed? The individual who has developed the 2nd stage of Arūpa Jhāna, having seen the faults of this Jhāna and good results of the 3rd Jhāna, eradicates the 2nd Jhāna and with a view to developing the 3rd Jhāna, takes for his object the non-existence of the consciousness of 1st Jhāna and practices the exercise repeating natthi kinci (නත්ථි කිඤ්චි) or there is naught whatever. To one who so does, when the hindrances are completely inhibited, the 3rd stage of Arūpa Jhāna supervenes (ākincaññāyatana Kusala cittan ආකිඤ්චඤ්ඤායතන කුසල චිත්තං).

4TH JHĀNA.

To him who practises the preliminary exercise on the cognition of the 3rd Arūpa stage, mentally repeating 'This is calm', 'This is excellent,' the 4th stage of Arūpa Jhāna supervenes. In any consciousness in full ecstasy (samāpatti සමාපත්ති) there is no perception from the view point of grossness, and there is perception from the view point of subtlety. That consciousness in full ecstasy (samāpatti සමාපත්ති) is called the 4th Arūpa Jhāna of neither perception nor no perception (Nēvasaññā nāsaññāyatana Kusala cittan නෙවසඤ්ඤා නාසඤ්ඤායතන කුසල චිත්තං). It is like the vessel that contained oil and emptied, as one is not quite accurate if he states there is oil or there is no oil. How can this 4th Jhāna be developed? The individual who had developed the 3rd stage of Arūpa Jhāna, having seen the faults of this Jhāna and the good effects of the 4th Jhāna, takes for his object consciousness of the 3rd stage of Arūpa Jhāna and practises repeating the formulas "This is calm, This is excellent" (Santamētan paneetamētan සන්තමෙතං පණීතමෙතං) and duly develops the 4th stage of Arūpa

Jhāna (Nēvāsaññā nāsaññāyatana Kusala cittan නෙවසඤ්ඤා නාසඤ්ඤායතන කුසල චිත්තං).

RESULTANT CONSCIOUSNESS OF EACH OF THE FOUR OBJECTS OF THOUGHT.

Resultant consciousness of each of the four objects of thought resembles those classes of moral consciousness dwelling on the infinity of space etc. The only difference being one resultant effects and the other good kamma.

1. After developing the 1st Stage of Arūpa Jhāna if one were to die in that ecstasy he is reborn in the sphere of the conception of infinite space, where the life-term is 20,000 great kappas (aeons). Rebirth consciousness, life continuum and redecease, there, is the resultant consciousness of the infinity of space.

2. Having developed the 2nd stage of Arūpa Jhāna, if one were to die in ecstasy, he is reborn in the sphere of the conception of infinite consciousness, where the life term is 40,000 great kappas (aeons). Resultant consciousness of infinite consciousness exists there by way of rebirth life-continuum and re-decease.

3. Having developed the 3rd stage of Arūpa Jhāna, if one were to die in ecstasy, he is reborn in the sphere of the conception of nothingness, where the life term is 60,000 great kappas (aeons). Resultant consciousness of nothingness exists there by way of rebirth, life-continuum and re-decease.

4. Having developed the 4th stage of Arūpa Jhāna, if one were to die in ecstasy he is reborn in the sphere of neither consciousness, nor unconsciousness, where the life term is 80,000 great kappas (aeons). Resultant consciousness of neither consciousness nor unconsciousness exists there by way of rebirth, life-continuum and redecease.

INEFFECTIVE CONSCIOUSNESS OF EACH OF THE FOUR OBJECTS OF THOUGHTS.

These four classes of consciousness resemble the four classes of moral consciousness dwelling on the infinity of space and so on. Moral classes arise in the worldlings (puthujjana පුථුජ්ජන) and those who have entered the first three paths and gained the first three fruits. Ineffective classes arise only in Arahats. When an Arahat develops the 1st stage of Arūpa Jhāna then that consciousness is called Ineffective consciousness dwelling on the infinity of space, and so on with the other three stages.

> Ālambanappabhēdēna catuddhāruppa mānasan
> Puññapāka Kriyābhēdā punadvādasadhāṭhitan.
>
> ආලම්බනප්පභෙදෙන චතුධාරුප්ප මානසං
> පුඤ්ඤපාක ක්‍රියාභෙදා පුනද්වාදසධාඨිතං
>
> " Four kinds of mental objects may be sought,
> In mind rapt in Arūpalōka thought,
> Classed as to merit, or as just effect,
> Or bringing none, twelve fold will be correct. "

THE EIGHT ECSTASIES.

When the five stages of Jhāna in Rūpalōka are taken as four, they together with the four stages of Arūpa Jhāna are called the eight ecstasies (අට්ඨසමාපත්ති aṭṭhaSamāpatti). When Lord Buddha preached the doctrine to very wise and intelligent people, he described as four Jhānas in Rūpalōka, and to the less intelligent ones as five Jhānas.

SUPERNORMAL KNOWLEDGE.

Now, if one has emerged from the fifth stage of Jhāna, the foundation for supernormal knowledge. (Abhiññā අභිඤ්ඤා), and performs the preliminary exercise of meditations on the phenomenon determined on, for instance, in order to develop " The powers of Iddhi ", he repeats the formula Satan hōmi Sahassan hōmi (සතං හොමි සහස්සං හොමි) and so on, then the fifth stage of Jhāna proceeding by way of that knowledge supervenes with a visible or other object as its object according to circumstances. In the instance quoted above the individual appears as one hundred or one thousand beings resembling him, if he had so willed. By supernormal knowledge is meant (1) The powers named Iddhi (Iddhividhagñānaya ඉද්ධිවිධඥානය), (2) The celestial ear (dibba sōta දිබ්බසොත), (3) Discerning others' thoughts (paracitta vijānana පරචිත්ත විජානන) (4) Reminiscence of former births (pubbē nivāsānussati පුබ්බෙ

නිවාසානුස්සති) and (5) The Heavenly Eye (dibba cakkhu දිබ්බ චක්ඛු). By Iddhi many a phenomenon could be induced, such as diving in the earth as in water, walking or flying in the air, walking in water as on earth, touching the moon or the sun etc. The reader should consult Paṭisambhidā Magga (Mahāvagga ñana kathā) for more information in respect of inducing supernormal knowledge (අභිඤ්ඤා, Abhiññā). In each case one has to begin by so exercising himself in the four steps to Iddhi, that mind and body become perfected in training wholly in subjection, pliant and adaptable to the will. Reminiscence of former births is acquired by meditation on the Paṭicca Samuppāda.

EXERCISES SUITABLE FOR DEVELOPING

5TH JHĀNA.

The suitable exercises for developing the 5th stage of Jhāna are the ten hypnotic (Kasina කසිණ) circles, exercise in respiration and equanimity, the last of the four illimitables or sublime abodes.

PEOPLE CAPABLE OF DEVELOPING

5TH JHĀNA.

Fifth Jhāna can be cultivated only by people whose rebirth consciousness is associated with the three hētus (හේතු) of disinterestedness, amity and knowledge amounting to in-sight (Tihētuka paṭisandhi puggalō තිහේතුක පටිසන්ධිපුග්ගලෝ). Those who have practised mental culture in the round of births will find no difficulty and, as a matter of fact, will with ease be able to attain the 5th stage of Jhāna, in any existence they are born with a Tihētuka paṭisandhi (තිහේතුක පටිසන්ධි) provided they are not hindered by bad Kamma, torments and bad resultant effects of previous bad kamma and they associate themselves with teachers who have developed the 5th stage of Jhāna and who are able to give the necessary exercise according to his character.

CHAPTER VI.

TRANSCENDENTAL CONSCIOUSNESS.

4. Transcendental (supramundane) consciousness[1].

Of consciousness in the paths and fruition there are four classes of consciousness which are transcendental and moral, to wit :—

1. Consciousness belonging to the path of stream-attainment.
2. Consciousness belonging to the path of once-returning.
3. Consciousness belonging to the path of Never-returning.
4. Consciousness belonging to the path of Arahatship.

NOTE 1.

Lōkuttara (ලෝකුත්තර) literally beyond the worlds, that is, beyond the world of five aggregates (Pancakkhandā).

Next, there are four classes of transcendental resultant consciousness, to wit :—

5-8 Consciousness belonging to the fruition of each of the abovenamed four paths.

These, summed up, amount in all, to eight classes of consciousness, both moral and resultant, arising in transcendental thought.

CONSCIOUSNESS BELONGING TO THE 1ST PATH.

Consciousness belonging to the path of stream-attainment is Sōtapatti magga cittan (සෝතාපත්ති මග්ග චිත්තං) Sōta (සෝත) is a stream of water. The eight fold āriyan path is called the stream, because it leads to the great Ocean called Nibbāna. Attainment for the first time of the stream called the Eight Fold āriyan path is known as stream-attainment. The consciousness of the 1st Path obtained therefrom is known as consciousness belonging to the Path of stream attainment (Sōtapatti magga cittan සොතාපත්ති මග්ග චිත්තං). Or it may be that the individual, who for the first time attains the stream known as the Eight Fold āriyan path, is stream-winner (සොතාපත්ති Sōtapatti), and his consciousness of the path is Sōtapatti magga cittan (සොතාපත්ති මග්ග චිත්තං). Consciousness of the 1st Path is that which totally extirpates or annihilates three of the fetters *viz* erroneous views regarding self, doubt and practice of wrongful rites and ceremonies.

The individual who attains the 1st path realizes Nibbāna only to such an extent as seeing a golden vessel in a dark room by the aid of a flash of lightning. He totally annihilates five classes of immoral consciousness and the remaining seven classes are so attenuated as to prevent him from being reborn in the four planes of misery, just as a tree that has been struck by lightning and whose branches and so on have been damaged is unable to exist for a considerable period. If he does not attain Arahatship in that existence, he will do so after being reborn seven times or earlier in the happier forms of Kāmalōka existence. If he attains Arahatship in the next existence he is known as ēkabeejee (එකබීජී), if in the seventh existence sattakkhattu paramō (සත්තක්ඛත්තු පරමො) and if in the interval between the two Kōlan Kōla (කොලං කොල).

CONSCIOUSNESS BELONGING TO THE 2ND PATH.

Consciousness belonging to the path of once-returning is Sakadāgāmi magga cittan (සකදාගාමි මග්ග චිත්තං). Sakin āgāmi — Sakadāgāmi (සකිං ආගාමි — සකදාගාමි) is once-returning. Consciousness of the path of the once-returner is Sakadāgāmi magga cittan (සකදාගාමි මග්ග චිත්තං). The individual who has attained the 2nd path realizes Nibbāna to such a degree as seeing a golden vessel in a dark room by the aid of a lamp light. At the moment of entering the 2nd Path, lust, hate and nescience lying dormant, become attenuated.

1. Having attained the path of once-returning, one can in this existence itself become an Arahat and attain Pari Nibbāna.

2. Attaining the path of once-returning in this existence, and being reborn in another place of existence, one can become an Arahat and attain Pari Nibbāna.

3. One can attain the path of once-returning in another existence and there itself become an Arahat and attain Pari Nibbāna.

4. Having attained the path of once-returning in another existence and being reborn in this existence, one can become an Arahat and obtain Pari Nibbāna.

5. Attaining the path of once-returning in this existence, and being reborn in another place of existence and being again reborn in this existence, one can attain Arahatship and reach Pari Nibbāna. Thus, the once-returner is of five types. It is in consideration of the 5th type that he is called a once-returner. Once-returner is in reality the one who has gained fruition in the 2nd path but for the purpose of knowing the distinctions it has been so stated.

CONSCIOUSNESS BELONGING TO THE 3RD PATH.

Consciousness belonging to the path of never-returning is Anāgāmi magga cittan (අනාගාමි මග්ග චිත්තං). Na āgāmi —Anāgāmi (න ආගාමි—අනාගාමි) by way of rebirth one who does not return to the Kāmalōka is known as Never-returner. This consciousness belonging to the path of Never-returning is known as Anāgāmi magga cittan (අනාගාමි මග්ග චිත්තං). He realizes Nibbāna as if he saw the golden vessel referred to above by moonlight. At that moment the two fetters of lust and hate that were lying dormant in an attenuated state are completely annihilated and extinguished. If he does not become an Arahat in this existence itself, he will be reborn in the pure Abodes of Brahamalōka and attain Arahatship there. He will never be reborn in this existence.

CONSCIOUSNESS BELONGING TO THE 4TH PATH.

Consciousness belonging to the path of Arahatship is Arahatta magga cittan (අරහත්ත මග්ග චිත්තං). He is called Arahat, because the word Arahan (අරහං) fittest, is an attribute present in him. Because he is the fittest person to receive offerings of any kind from people in the worlds of men, Dēvas and Brahmas, also because he exterminated the round of births by utterly destroying all the Torments, and annihilated the fires of lust, ill-will and nescience and also because he even secretly never commits a bad deed, he is called an Arahat. His consciousness belonging to the path of Arahatship is known as Arahatta magga cittan (අරහත්ත මග්ග චිත්තං). One who has attained this consciousness has realized Nibbāna as if he saw the golden vessel referred to above by the light of the Sun when it is at its zenith. At that moment the subtle defilements and torments lying dormant are completely destroyed and annihilated. After death he will no more be reborn in any place of existence and attain the peace of Pari Nibbāna.

CONSCIOUSNESS BELONGING TO THE FRUITION OF THE FOUR PATHS.

Consciousness belonging to the fruition of each of the four paths are [1]Resultant consciousness of the 1st path (Sōtāpatti phala cittan සොතාපත්ති ඵල චිත්තං).

2. Resultant consciousness of the 2nd path (Sakadāgāmi phala cittan සකදාගාමි ඵල චිත්තං).

3. Resultant consciousness of the 3rd path (Anāgāmi phala cittan අනාගාමි ඵල චිත්තං).

4. Resultant consciousness of the 4th path (Arahatta phala cittan අරහත්ත ඵල චිත්තං).

RESULTANT CONSCIOUSNESS OF THE 1ST PATH.

1. Resultant consciousness of the 1st path is that state of consciousness immediately following the one belonging to the path of stream attainment and is called the sōtāpatti phala cittan (සොතාපත්ති ඵල චිත්තං). Consciousness of the path is moral, and resultant consciousness should be understood as the resulting effects or fruition of the path. The resulting

effects of moral consciousness in Kāmalōka and soon occur either in the same existence or any other future existences after lapse of time. The resulting effects or fruition of transcendental consciousness (lōkōttara ලොකොත්තර) take place at the very next moment following Path consciousness. Hence Akāliko (අකාලිකො) one of the attributes of the Dhamma.

RESULTANT CONSCIOUSNESS OF THE 2ND PATH.

Consciousness immediately following that belonging to the path of once-returning is the fruition or resulting effects of the path of once-returning (Sakadāgāmi phala cittan සකදාගාමි ඵල චිත්තං). Here too the path is moral consciousness and fruition is the resulting effects.

RESULTANT CONSCIOUSNESS OF THE 3RD PATH.

Consciousness immediately following that belonging to the path of never-returning is the fruition or resulting effects of the path of never-returning (Anāgāmi phala cittan අනාගාමි ඵල චිත්තං). Here too the path is moral consciousness and fruition is the resulting effects.

RESULTANT CONSCIOUSNESS OF THE 4TH PATH.

Resultant consciousness immediately following the one belonging to the path of Arahatship is the fruition or resulting effects of the path of Arahatship (Arahatta phala cittan අරහත්ත ඵල චිත්තං). Here too, the path is moral and fruition the result.

These four classes of transcendental moral consciousness arise only once and never twice, and therfore there is no class of transcendental ineffective consciousness (lōkōttara kriya cittan ලොකොත්තර ක්‍රියා චිත්තං).

FUNCTIONS OF THE FOUR PATHS.

Each of the paths performs four functions at one and the same time (1) discerning the truth of suffering (2) expelling the truth of its cause (3) realising the truth of its cessation and (4) cultivating the truth of the way to cessation. How four functions can be performed at the same moment is explained by the following illustration of lighting an oil lamp. When an oil lamp is lit, four phenomena occur *viz* (1) disappearance of darkness (2) diffusion of light (3) extinction of oil and (4) extinction of the wick, at the same moment. In each of the paths it is (the cētasikapaññā) knowledge amounting to insight coexisting in the class of consciousness belonging to the paths that acts as the light which realizes the four āriyan truths. After the Path-consciousness two or three moments of consciousness of fruition take place according to the degree of insight in the individual, after which there comes subsidence into the life continuum. Then again the life continuum is interrupted and the knowledges concerned with " review " (paccavekkhana ñanāni පචච වෙකඛණ ඤාණානි) occur. The individual who has gained the fruition of the first three paths does not realise the four āriyan truths just like the reappearance of darkness after extinguishing the light of a lamp. But in the case of one who has gained the fruition of the path belonging to Arahatship, the cētasika paññā (චෙතසික පඤඤා) coexisting therein remains always the same realising the four āriyan truths right through the rest of his life till he attains Pari Nibbāna.

NOTE 1.

Paccavekkhana ñanāni (පචච වෙකඛණ ඤාණානි). The āriya now (1) reviews the path he has just attained (2) the fruit of that path he has just enjoyed (3) the Nibbāna he has intuited, though not quite realised, as an object of the consciousness of the path and of fruition. The remaining torments (upakkilēsas උපක්කිලෙස) he may or may not realise.

" Catumaggappabhēdēna catuddhā kusalan tathā
Pākan tassa phalattāti aṭṭhadhānuttaran matan "

චතුමගගපපභෙදෙන චතුඩා කුසලං තථා
පාකං තසස ඵලතතාති අඪධානුතතරං මතං

" Four are the paths, hence, four kinds of thoughts,
Four fruits, hence, four resultant kinds we're taught,
Eight states in all when highest things are ought. "

SUMMARY OF CLASSES OF CONSCIOUSNESS

" Dvādasākusalānēvan kusalānēka vīsati
Chattinsēva vipākāni kriyācittani vīsati "

වාදසාකුසලානෙවං කුසලානෙක වීසති
ඡත්තිංසෙව විපාකානි ක්‍රියාචිත්තානි වීසති

12 classes of immoral consciousness
21 classes of moral consciousness
36 classes of resultant consciousness
20 classes of ineffective consciousness
89

Catupaññāsadhā kāmē—Rūpē pannarasīrayē
Cittāni dvādasāruppē—aṭṭhadhānuttarē tathā

චතුපඤ්ඤසධා කාමෙ—රූපෙ පන්නරසීරයෙ
චිත්තානි වාදසාරූප්පෙ—අට්ඨධානුත්තරෙ තථා

54 classes of consciousness in Kāmalōka
15 classes of consciousness in Rūpalōka
12 classes of consciousness in Arūpalōka
8 classes of transcendental consciousness
89

" Itthamēkūnanavutippabhēdan pana mānasan
Ekavīsasatan vātha vibhajanti vicakkhanā "

ඉත්ථමෙකූනනවුතිප්පභෙදං පන මානසං
ඒකවීසසතං වාථවිභජන්ති විචක්ඛණා

Here the 89 classes of consciousness are analyzed into 121 classes by seers.

How can consciousness that is analyzed into eightynine come to have one hundred and twenty one classes?

TRANSCENDENTAL CONSCIOUSNESS BECOMING FORTY.

By resolving each of the eight kinds of transcendental consciousness into five, thus obtaining forty kinds in place of eight.

In the path of stream-attainment there is a class of consciousness for each of the five stages of Jhāna. In the path of once-returning there is a class of consciousness for each of the five stages of Jhāna. So for the path of never-returning and of Arahatship, making twenty classes of path consciousness in all. Similarly there are twenty classes of fruition consciousness; and these together make forty classes of transcendental consciousness.

1. In the path of stream-attainment there is a class of consciousness accompanied by initial application, sustained application, pleasurable interest, pleasure and one pointedness.

2. In the path of stream-attainment there is a class of consciousness accompanied by sustained application, pleasurable interest, pleasure and one pointedness.

3. In the path of stream-attainment there is a class of consciousness accompanied by pleasurable interest, pleasure and one pointedness.

4. In the path of stream-attainment there is a class of consciousness accompanied by pleasure and one pointedness.

5. In the path of stream attainment there is a class of consciousness accompanied by hedonic indifference and one pointedness. Similarly five classes in the path of once-returning, five in the path of never-returning and five in the path of Arahatship.

THREE WAYS OF COUNTING TRANSCENDENTAL CONSCIOUSNESS

There are three ways of counting the classes of transcendental consciousness by way of Jhāna *viz* (1) pādaka Jhāna (**පාදක ඣාන**) (2) Sammasita Jhāna (**සම්මසිත ඣාන**) and (3) Puggala jjhāsa Jhāna (**පුග්ගල ජ්ඣාස ඣාන**).

(1) If one, who has cultivated the Jhānas, at first were to induce the 1st stage of Jhāna and emerging therefrom contemplate all conditioned things as impermanent, ill and soul-less and attain the path of stream-attainment, his consciousness belonging to the path is called the path consciousness of stream-attainment by way of 1st Jhāna (paṭhamajjhāna sōtāpatti magga cittan පඨමජ්ඣාන සොතාපත්ති මග්ග චිත්තං and consciousness of fruition, resultant consciousness of stream-attainment by way of 1st Jhāna (patthamajjhāna sōtāpatti phala cittan පඨමජ්ඣාන සොතාපත්ති ඵල චිත්තං). In like manner by way of 2nd Jhāna and so on, and similarly in regard to Path-consciousness of once-returning and so on. This is by way of Pādakajjhāna (පාදකජ්ඣාන) inducing Jhāna. (2) If one without inducing the 1st Jhāna, were merely to contemplate the factors of the 1st Jhāna such as initial application and so on as impermanent, ill and soul-less, and attain the Path-consciousness of stream-attainment, his consciousness is also known as paṭhamajjhāna sōtāpatti magga cittan (පඨමජ්ඣාන සොතාපත්ති මග්ග චිත්තං) and consciousness of fruition pathamajjhāna phala cittan (පඨමජ්ඣාන ඵල චිත්තං). Similarly with the rest. This is by way of contemplation without inducing Jhāna (සම්මසිතජ්ඣාන) Sammasitajjhāna.

(3). If one, who has cultivated the Jhānas, having induced the 1st Jhāna or maintained the 1st Jhāna were to awake therefrom and contemplate the factors of the 2nd Jhāna and so on as transient, ill and soul-less or having no substantial entity, he would attain the path consciousness according to his wishes. It is thus:—if he were to wish that he should attain the path consciousness from the 1st Jhāna he has induced, then he would so attain the path. Or else, if he were to wish that he should attain the path consciousness from the factors of the Jhāna, he would contemplate the factors of the Jhāna without inducing same as transient, ill and soul-less and then attain the path. Similarly in regard to the other Paths. This is by way of the wishes of the person (puggalajjhāsa පුග්ගලජ්ඣාස).

DIFFERENTIATION OF CLASSES ACCORDING TO JHANA FACTORS.

1. " Jhānangayōgabhēdēna Katvē Kēkantu pancadhā,
Vuccatānuttaran cittan cattālisa vidhantica."

2. " Yathāca rūpāvacaran gaihatānuttaran tathā
Paṭhamādi Jhānabhēdē āruppaneāpi pancamē

3. " Ekādasavidhan tasmā pathamādi Kameeritan
Jhānamēkēkamantētu tēveesatividhan bhavē "

4. Sattatinsavidhan puññan dvipaññāsa vidhan tathā
pākamiccāhu cittani ekaveesa satan budhāthi."

1. ඣානඞ්ගයොග හෙදෙන කතෙව් කෙකන්තු පචධා
වුච්චතානුත්තරං. චිත්තං. චත්තාලිස විධන්තිච

2. යථාච රූපාවචරං ගය්හතානුත්තරං තථා
පඨමාදි ඣානහෙදෙ ආරුප්පචාපි පචමෙ

3 එකාදසවිධං තස්මා පඨමාදි කම්රිතං.
ඣානමෙකෙකමන්තතු තෙවීසතිවිධං. භවෙ

4. සත්තතිංසවිධං පුඤ්ඤං ද්වීපඤ්ඤාසවිධං තථා
පාකමිච්චාහු චිත්තානි එකවීස සතං.බුධාති

Distinguishing the Jhāna of each path as well as stage, and when multiplied by five, classes of transcendental consciousness are stated to be forty.

When reckoned in this manner, classes of consciousness of Arūpalōka are included in the 5th stage of Jhāna as the factors are the same. The 5th stage of Jhāna is accompanied by hedonic indifference and one pointedness and such is the case with consciousness of Arūpalōka.

Therefore, we have 11 classes of consciousness belonging to the 1st Jhāna, 3 by way of Rūpalōka (worldly) and 8 by way of transcendental (beyond the world). Similarly the number in the 2nd stage of Jhāna is 11, 3rd stage 11, and 4th stage 11. In the 5th stage of Jhāna there are 23 in all, that is 15 by way of worldly consciousness as the 12 classes in Arūpalōka are included here, and 8 by way of transcendental (beyond the world).

According to this manner of calculation classes of moral consciousness are 37 (kāmalōka 8, rupalōka 5, arūpalōka 4, and transcendental 20), resultant consciousness 52 (kāmalōka without hētus 15 and with hētus 8, rūpalōka 5, arūpalōka 4, and transcendental 20), and ineffective consciousness 20 as stated before. They are as follows :—

(*a*)	classes of	immoral	consciousness	12
(*b*)	do	moral	do	37
(*c*)	do	resultant	do	52
(*d*)	do	inoperative	do	20
			TOTAL	121

PART II.

CHAPTER VII

MENTAL PROPERTIES.

" Ekuppāda nirōdhāca ēkālambana vatthukā
cētoyuttā dvipaññāsa dhammācētasikā matā."

එකුප්පාද නිරොධාච එකාලම්බන වත්ථුකා
චෙතොයුත්තා ද්විපඤ්ඤාස ධම්මාචෙතසිකා මතා

Allied to thought are two and fifty states called mental properties.[1] They arise and cease with it, and share its object and its base. How are they distinguished?

MENTAL PROPERTIES COMMON TO ALL CLASSES.

I. There are seven Mental properties which are common to every act of consciousness to wit :—

(1) Contact (phassō ඵස්සො).
(2) Feeling (Vēdanā වෙදනා).
(3) perception (Saññā සඤ්ඤා).
(4) Volition[2] (cētanā චෙතනා).
(5) one-pointedness (ēkaggatā ඒකග්ගතා).
(6) psychic life (Jīvitindriyan ජීවිතින්ද්‍රියං).
(7) attention[3] (manasikārō මනසිකාරො).

NOTE 1.

Cētasikā (චෙතසිකා) derived from cētō (චෙතො) which is consciousness, thought or mind. In any section of conscious experience citta (චිත්ත) is distinguished from its concomitants, that is, all the mental factors or elements distinguishable in the fact of conscious or subjective experience. Several mental factors combine in consciousness to constitute a state of consciousness (cittuppāda චිත්තුප්පාද.)

NOTE 2.

Cētanā (චේතනා) is derived from the verb cēteti (චේතේති), literally, think.

NOTE 3.

The Venerable Buddhaghosa explains (1) (7) as follows :—Manasikārō (මනසිකාරෝ) means acting (kiriyakārō කිරියකාරෝ), making with respect to consciousness (manō මනෝ) making consciousness one's field as if it were a previous consciousness. Manasikārō (මනසිකාරෝ) has three modes, according as it is concerned with object, sense, procedure or apperceptions. In the last two it is synonymous with the mind "turning towards" sensation or idea respectively. Here only the first mode is meant, and here it means movement of mind confronting its object and passing it on like a driver to whatever it is connected "withal". Hence attention is the constant element of selective co-ordinating consciousness, and the variable element of mental strain or tension, consciously felt and connoted is initial and sustained application.

THE FOUR CHARACTERISTICS OF MENTAL PROPERTIES.

There are 52 states or mental properties associated with or coexisting in consciousness, such as contact, feeling, perception and so on. They are said to be associated with or coexisting in consciousness as they possess four characteristics namely, of arising and ceasing with consciousness and having the same object and the base as consciousness. Of the three phases of a state of consciousness *viz* arising (uppāda උප්පාද), static period (ඨිති ṭhiti) and ceasing (bhanga භංග), it is at the instant of the arising of consciousness that the associated or coexisting states arise, neither an instant before nor after. This is the characteristic of arising. At the instant of ceasing of consciousness the associated states cease, neither before nor after. This is the characteristic of ceasing. Consciousness arises from the two correlations of object and sufficing condition in object. Objects are of six kinds *viz* a visual object, auditory object (hearing), olfactory object (smell), gustatory object (taste), a tactile object (touch) and cognizable object (concept or idea). These six kinds may be objects of the past, present, and future. Sufficing condition in object is that to which weight is attached. There are also freed from time such states as term and concept (paññatti පඤ්ඤත්ති), that which makes things known or that which is made known, consciousness and its mental concomitants called mind, both personal or internal, and external and Nibbāna. Consciousness arises through the help of the two correlations taking for its object anyone of the above mentioned states. The associated or coexisting mental properties too take the same object beginning from a visual object and ending in Nibbāna as consciousness. This is the characteristic of having one object. The two classes of cognition of eye arise having the sensitive material quality of the eye for its base. The associated mental properties such as contact and so on which are common to all classes of consciousness present in those two classes of cognition of the eye, have for their base the sensitive material quality of the eye. The elements of cognitions of ear, nose, tongue and body should be similarly understood as stated in respect of eye-base. The element of mind and the element of mind-cognition which comprise the remaining 79 classes of consciousness have for their base the heart-base. The mental properties associated with or coexisting in those classes of consciousness have for their base the heart-base. This is the characteristic of having one base. These are the four characteristics associated with mental properties.

In the sentence " සුඛාය වෙදනාය සම්පයුත්තො ධම්මො " (sukhāya vēdanāya sampayuttō dhammō) preached by The Lord Buddha, " sañ සං " signifies " neither before nor after " and the mind and its mental concomitants arise at one and the same time, and " pa ප " signifies the four characteristics described above.

REASONS FOR CALLING THEM CĒTASIKĀ OR MENTAL PROPERTIES.

" cittēna sahavattatīti cētasikō,
cētasiniyuttan vā cētasikan "
**"චිත්තෙන සහවත්තතීති චෙතසිකො,
චෙතසිනියුත්තං වා චෙතසිකං".**

According to the meaning of the above, they are called cētasikā or mental properties because they arise coexisting in consciousness or mind, and they are associated with consciousness or mind. If such be the case it can be questioned as to why material quality arising from mind is not called a cētasika or mental property. The answer is that such material qualities arising from mind do not bear the four characteristics above stated. The material quality arising from mind has one characteristic resembling the mind, namely, that of arising at the same instant, but do not resemble the mind in respect of the two characteristics of ceasing and having one object. A question can be asked as to why kāya viññatti and vacī viññatti (කායවිඤ්ඤත්ති වචී විඤ්ඤත්ති) the two material qualities of media of communication through body and speech, which resemble consciousness in the fact of arising and ceasing as stated in the duals චිත්තානුපරිවත්තිනො ධම්මා චිත්ත සහභූනො ධම්මා ("cittānuparivattinō dhammā, citta sahabhūnō dhammā") are not included among cētasikas or mental properties. Those two material qualities though resembling in two characteristics, do not resemble in respect of object and base. Therefore they should not be included among the cētasikas or mental properties. A moment of consciousness has three instants *viz* arising (uppāda උප්පාද stationary (ṭhiti ඨිති) and ceasing bhanga භංග). With the exception of the material qualities of media of communication the rest of the material qualities originating from mind last till the lapse of 51 such instants or 17 moments of thought or consciousness. That is not all ; material qualities originating from mind are unable to conceive objects. Consciousness is able to conceive objects. Again, classes of consciousness are associated with such bases as eye-base and so on. The material qualities derived from the four great essentials (upādā rūpa උපාදාරූප) and originating from mind are, in each group (kalāpa කලාප) associated with the four great essentials existing in each group. Therefore material qualities, which, originating from mind, though resembling a consciousness only in the characteristic of arising, do not resemble in the other three characteristics in respect of ceasing at one and the same time and having one object and one base, cannot be included among the cētasikas or mental properties.

II. Next, there are six mental properties termed particular[1] (not invariably present in consciousness) to wit :—

MENTAL PROPERTIES

CALLED PARTICULAR.

(1) Initial application (vitakkō විතක්කො).
(2) Sustained application (vicārō විචාරො).
(3) Deciding (Adhimokkhō අධිමොක්ඛො).
(4) Effort (viriyan විරියං).
(5) Pleasurable interest (pīti පීති).
(6) Conation desire-to-do (chandō ඡන්දො).[2]

Now these 13 mental properties are to be considered as being either one or the other.

NOTE 1.

Pakinnakā (පකිණ්ණකා) lit: scattered about.

NOTE 2.

Kattu kammyatā chanda (කත්තු කම්‍යතා ඡන්ද is intended here.)

NOTE 3.

Añña samānā (අඤ්ඤ සමානා).
They are purely psychological terms of immoral import, but become moral or immoral, according as they combine in a moral or immoral thought.

III. Next, there are 14 immoral mental properties, to wit :—

IMMORAL MENTAL PROPERTIES.

(1) Dulness (mōhō මොහො)
(2) Impudence (ahirikan අහිරිකං)
(3) Recklessness of consequences (anottappan අනොත්තප්පං)
(4) Distraction (uddhacchañ උද්ධච්චං
(5) Greed (lōbhō ලොභො)

(6) Error (diṭṭhi දිට්ඨි)
(7) Conceit (mānō මානො)
(8) Hate (dōsō දොසො)
(9) Envy (issā ඉස්සා)
(10) Selfishness (macchariyan මච්ඡරියං)
(11) Worry (kukkuccan කුක්කුච්චං)
(12) Sloth (thīnan ථීනං)
(13) Torpor (middhan මිද්ධං)
(14) Perplexity (vicikicchā විචිකිච්ඡා)

IV. Next, there are nineteen mental properties which are common to all that is moral and beautiful to wit :—

MENTAL PROPERTIES COMMON TO ALL THAT IS BEAUTIFUL.[1]

(1) Confidence (saddhā සද්ධා)
(2) Mindfulness (sati සති)
(3) Prudence (hiri හිරි)
(4) Discretion (ottappan ඔත්තප්පං)
(5) Disinterestedness (alōbhō අලොභො)
(6) Amity (adōso අදොසො)
(7) Balance of mind (tatramajjatthatā තත්‍රමජ්ඣත්තතා)
(8) Composure of mental properties[2] (kāyapassaddhi කාය පස්සද්ධි)
(9) Composure of mind (citta-passaddhi චිත්තපස්සද්ධි)
(10) Buoyancy of mental properties (kāya lahutā කාය ලහුතා)
(11) Buoyancy of mind (citta lahutā චිත්තලහුතා)
(12) Pliancy of mental properties (kāya mudutā කාය මුදුතා)
(13) Pliancy of mind (cittamudutā චිත්තමුදුතා)
(14) Fitness of work of mental properties (kāya kammaññatā කායකම්මඤ්ඤතා)
(15) Fitness of work of mind (චිත්තකම්මඤ්ඤතා citta kammaññatā)
(16) Proficiency of mental properties (kāya pāguññatā කායපාගුඤ්ඤතා)
(17) Proficiency of mind (citta pāguññatā චිත්තපාගුඤ්ඤතා)
(18) Rectitude of mental properties (kayujjukatā කායුජ්ජු) කතා
(19) Rectitude of mind (cittujjukatā චිත්තුජ්ජුකතා)

NOTE 1.

Sōbhana sādhāranā (සොභනසාධාරණ) common to all that is beautiful.

NOTE 2.

Kāya (කාය) here, meaning aggregate, refers to the nāma kāya (නාමකාය) as opposed to the rūpa kāya (රූපකාය). That it is so can be seen from the following comment kayōtiti cettha vēdanādi khandhattayassa gahanan (කායොතීති චෙත්ථ වේදනාදිඛන්ධත්තයස්ස ගහණං) This agress with The Venerable Buddhaghosa's Attha Sālini Kāya (කාය) means the three khandas (ඛන්ධ) feeling (vēdanā වෙදනා), perception (saññā සඤ්ඤා) and volitional activities (sankhārā සංඛාරා) Hence the distinction appears to be, not so much between sense of thought, as between factors of consciousness and consciousness as a whole.

V. Next, there are three Abstinences,[1] *viz*:—

THE THREE ABSTINENCES.

(1) Right speech (sammāvācā සම්මාවාචා)
(2) Right action (sammā kammantō සම්මාකම්මන්තො)
(3) Right livelihood (sammā jīvō සම්මාජීවො)

NOTE 1.

Viratiyō (විරතියො) lit :— abstinences, that is, "finding no pleasure in taking away life" (pānātipātā vēramani sikkhā padan පාණාතිපාතා වෙරමණී සික්ඛාපදං or pativiratō hōti පටිවිරතොහොති) etc.

THE ILLIMITABLES AND REASON.

VI. Next, there are the illimitables,[1] *viz*:—

(1) Pity (karunā කරුණා)
(2) Appreciation[2] (muditā මුදිතා)[2]

These, together with VII reason[3] (පඤ්ඤින්ද්‍රියං paññindriyan), in all manner of division, are to be considered as the twenty five morally beautiful mental properties.

NOTE 1.

Two of the four Brahmavihāras. The other two are represented by iv (6) amity for mettā (මෙත්තා) and iv (7) balance of mind, equanimity, impartiality for upēkkhā (උපෙක්ඛා).

NOTE 2.

Muditā (මුදිතා) is joy felt over other's success or over good work done; the congratulatory or benevolent attitude.

NOTE 3.

Paññindriyan පඤ්ඤින්ද්‍රියං as a cētasika (චෙතසික) is not confined to the lōkōttara citta (ලෝකොත්තර චිත්ත) only.

CHAPTER VIII

COMPARISON OF MENTAL PROPERTIES WITH DRUGS.

For example, say a Pharmacist has 52 kinds of drugs, of which 13 are ordinary drugs, 14 poisonous drugs and 25 specifics. He is not able to compound a mixture with only the drugs themselves. It is absolutely necessary to have pure unpolluted water for the purpose. According to the prescription he utilizes some of the drugs and makes a mixture with water. After the mixture is made it is not possible to separate the different drugs from the water. Hence they are associated with or coexisting in the water. When the water is drunk the drugs too are drunk. The bottle containing the mixture, has water and drugs co-existing therein and incapable of being separated therefrom. Results obtained from different mixtures vary according to the properties of drugs; cure is effected in respect of specifics and relief rendered with ordinary drugs. Consciousness and mental properties function in the same manner. Cētasikas (චෛතසික) are the properties associated with or co-existing in a state of consciousness. Consciousness is like the water, and mental properties or cētasikā are like the drugs associated with or co-existing in the water. When a state of consciousness arises certain mental properties belonging to that class of consciousness also arise. When consciousness ceases, mental properties too cease. When consciousness perceives a sense impression or conceive an idea the mental properties too perceive the same sense impression or conceive the same idea. When consciousness has for its base the eye base and so on, the mental properties too have the same base. Therefore, the natural elements such as contact and so on arising in consciousness and possessing the four characteristic features above mentioned are called mental properties or cētasikā. The characteristics of consciousness and its concomitants are varied and many. Consciousness is like a drug and cētasikā are like the properties of a drug. Just as the mental properties do not arise without a state of consciousness, so cannot consciousness arise without its mental properties. Though such be the case, it must not be misunderstood that all the mental properties arise in consciousness at one and the same time. According to the sense impression or idea only a certain number of mental properties arise according to the class of consciousness. That is the reason why consciousness becomes 89 or 121 classes.

The number of mental properties is 52; they are classified as follows :—

(1) Common to all classes of consciousness	7	aññā sāmānā 13
(2) Particular mental properties	6	
(3) Immoral mental properties	14	
	27	
(4) Common to all classes of moral consciousness	19	25 sōbhana or beautiful
(5) Abstinences	3	
(6) The Illimitables	2	
(7) Reason	1	
	52	

MENTAL PROPERTIES COMMON TO ALL CLASSES OF CONSCIOUSNESS.

Mental properties common to all classes of consciousness are described as follows :—

1. Contact.

Contact (phassō ඵස්සො) is a state of taking hold of an object, as by touch. It can be compared to the flow of saliva from the mouth of a man who sees another eating some acid fruit, or to the fear that arises in one's consciousness almost amounting to a thrilling sensation, on seeing a man up a high tree in the midst of young branches, or the numbness of the teeth that is experienced by a person who hears the unpleasant sound occasioned by the sharpening of an instrument on a whetstone on which sand is placed. From these illustrations contact should be understood as to how the object is got hold of, as by touch. When any object such as a visual one comes within the avenue of the six sensory organs such as eye-door and so on, that state, which causes the arising of a state of consciousness, by being present in it at one and the same time and with the other coexistent mental properties, of getting hold of an object as if by touch is called contact. It is likened to the rays of sun falling upon a wall. Though not associated with the object, it gets hold of the object as if by touch. According to the different names given to different classes of consciousness, contact associated with or coexisting in them bear different names. For instance, contact associated with eye cognition (cakku viññāna චක්ඛුවිඤ්ඤාණ) is called visual contact (cakku samphassa චක්ඛු සම්ඵස්ස). Similarly, auditory contact, olfactory contact, gustatory contact, tactile contact and mind contact in respect of the other organs. Therefore, as it is present in all classes of consciousness it is called sabba citta sadhārana සබ්බචිත්ත සාධාරණ).

2. FEELING.

Feeling (vēdanā වේදනා) is a state associated with consciousness which experiences the taste of an object. What consciousness is capable of doing is to perceive an object or conceive an idea. According to the object being pleasant, unpleasant and indifferent, there arises in consciousness pleasure, pain or indifference. Feeling is that state associated with consciousness which experiences the taste of an object. Therefore feeling is of three kinds *viz* pleasant and unpleasant and indifferent feeling.

The other mental properties too to a certain extent have the characteristic feature of experiencing the taste of an object, but not so prominently as feeling (vēdanā වේදනා). The latter has a dominating influence over others in respect of that feature. From the illustration "subhōjana rasassādako rājāviya" (සුභෝජන රසස්සාදකො රාජාවිය.) Both the cook and the king taste the food. The cook only experiences the taste by merely touching the food with the tongue, whereas the king by reason of his dominance will experience the taste during the whole period of his partaking of the food. Therefore feeling (vēdanā වේදනා) is like a king who experiences the taste of the food.

As feeling is also associated with the 89 classes of consciousness, it is called sabbacitta sādhārana (සබ්බ චිත්ත සාධාරණ), that is, it is common to all classes of consciousness

3. PERCEPTION.

Perception (saññā සඤ්ඤා) is that state associated with consciousness which perceives an object or which notes the nature of the object. It is like the carpenter who perceives the place where the timber should be sawn from, having previously made a mark ; or like noting same marks such as the colours white, red, blue or yellow in an object, but not able to give any reasons for the appearance of such colours. It is like a small child who, having seen a bull with two horns for the first time, on inquiring from his mother and coming to know that the animal is called a bull, notes that such an animal with two horns is a bull. But he does not know whether the bull was born of a cow, mare or she-elephant or originated from the earth. Therefore perception is that state associated with consciousness which perceives the object which has been previously seen by noting same marks. When consciousness too is associated with perception, he would know the characteristic features of mind and body, just as he would be knowing that the bull was born of a cow. When the faculty of reason is added to them, he would know that mind and body have the three salient features of impermanence, sorrow and soul-lessness which exist in all conditioned things, just like his being able to give more particulars about the origin of the bull, such as the country where it was brought from, breed etc. Consciousness thinks of the object. Perception associated with consciousness perceives or notes the nature of the object such as colour, shape, dimensions etc. If there is no perception in consciousness, it can only think but cannot note the nature of the object. Consciousness perceives and notes the nature of objects, because for some reason or other the property of perception is present in consciousness. This property of perception notes a mark the first time an object is seen, another mark the second time and so on for an indefinite period, the preceding mark being the cause of the succeeding ones.

In the five aggregates, the two aggregates of feeling and perception constitute these two mental properties feeling and perception. This perception too as it is associated with all the 89 classes of consciousness is called sabba citta sadhārana (සබ්බ චිත්ත සාධාරණ), that is, it is a property common to all classes of consciousness.

4. VOLITION.

Volition (cētanā චෙතනා) is that state or property associated with consciousness, which, whilst performing its function by way of willing in respect of the object, causes the other mental properties such as contact and so on which are associated with it, to perform their functions. It is like the teacher, who, whilst studying himself, causes his pupils to study their lessons, or the head carpenter, who, whilst doing his portion of the carpentry, makes his assistants do such work as has been entrusted to them.

Just as the owner of a paddy field going with a party of workmen to do some work in the field makes a greater effort than the others, in the same manner this volition makes a greater effort in performing its function than the other mental properties which are made to perform their functions each individually.

Volition which is associated with classes of moral and immoral consciousness is called Kamma (කම්ම), because it has the capacity to order and accumulate good or bad deeds.

This too is called, because it is associated with all classes of consciousness, a property common to all classes (sabba citta sādhārana සබ්බ චිත්ත සාධාරණ).

5. ONE-POINTEDNESS.

One-pointedness (ēkaggatā එකග්ගතා) is that property associated with each state of consciousness, which prevents the state of consciousness with its associated other mental properties from spreading on diverse objects and concentrating on each object and pointing to one object at a time. It is like the water, which prevents a quantity of powder, which is capable of spreading by fanning, from spreading and which keeps it 'en masse.'

Consciousness and the mental properties arise leaning on to one object only at a time. If this property is not associated with consciousness, then the consciousness and its mental properties would not be able to arise grasping one object at a time. When for some reason or other there is one-pointedness in consciousness, then consciousness and its mental properties arise pointing to and getting hold of one object. In some places that this one-pointedness is made known as concentration should be understood. This too, as it is associated with all the classes of consciousness, is called a mental property common to all classes of consciousness (sabba citta sādhārana සබබ චිතත සාධාරණ).

6. PSYCHIC LIFE.

Psychic life (Jīvitindriyañ ජීවිතින්‍ද්‍රියං) is a state associated with consciousness which prevents consciousness and its mental properties from dying. It maintains the life of consciousness and its mental properties. It is like the water that maintains the life of lotus and prevents it from fading.

If psychic life is not present in consciousness, then consciousness and its mental properties cannot exist and therefore die. It is because of the presence of psychic life in consciousness that consciousness and its mental properties exist without dying. On no occasion could the psychic life be separated from consciousness. It is present in every state of consciousness. Therefore, this too is a property common to all classes of consciousness (sabba citta sādhārana සබබ චිතත සාධාරණ). This is the psychic life of mind (nāma jīvitindriya නාමජීවිතින්‍ද්‍රිය). That of matter (rūpa jīvitindriya රූපජීවිතින්‍ද්‍රිය) will be discussed in the chapter on matter.

7. ATTENTION.

Attention (manasikārō මනසිකාරෝ) is that state which is present in every state of consciousness which moves the mind confronting its object, or that state which whilst confronting its object makes the associated mental properties too confront their object. It is like a driver of horses who directs them to go along the path he wishes. This property too is common to all classes of consciousness, as it is associated with all classes (sabba citta sādhārana සබබ චිතත සාධාරණ). Perception, volition, attention and application have very subtle differences. In some places "Five-door turning to" and "Mind-door turning to" are shown as attention.

As these 7 mental properties are associated with each class of consciousness described in chapter I, they are known as mental properties common to all classes (sabba citta sādhārana සබබ චිතත සාධාරණ).

CHAPTER IX

PARTICULAR MENTAL PROPERTIES.

1. INITIAL APPLICATION.

Initial application (vitakkō විතක්කො) is a state present in consciousness which makes consciousness and the associated mental properties reach an object and apply itself for the first time on an object. It is like an official accompanying a villager and visiting the king's palace. Here, initial application is like the official, consciousness is like the villager, and the object like the king's palace. Now, if there is no initial application, consciousness will not reach the object. Because there is this initial application in consciousness, consciousness reaches the object. As such is the case, the mental property present in consciousness, which makes consciousness reach an object, is called initial application.

In as much as a villager could reach the king's palace without an official, when he has got used to visiting the palace, so could consciousness, which has got used to reaching the object by initial application, reach an object later without initial application like classes of consciousness belonging to the 2nd. stage of Jhāna.

Right aspiration in the Eight-fold Noble Path is the initial application present in the transcendental classes of consciousness such as those of stream-attainment and so on. The initial application present in consciousness accompanied by insight is also right aspiration among those who are in the path of spiritual progress.

Initial application is obtained in 55 classes of consciousness *viz*. 44 classes of consciousness experienced in Kāmalōka with the exception of the twice five-fold sense impressions, and 11 classes of the 1st. stage of Jhāna. It is not associated with the 10 classes of twice five-fold sense impressions, 11 classes of the 2nd. stage of Jhāna, 11 of the 3rd. stage, 11 of the 4th. stage, and 23 of the 5th. stage of Jhāna, making in all 66 classes.

As initial application is a factor of Jhāna, the number of classes of consciousness with reference to this should be reckoned as 121.

2. SUSTAINED APPLICATION.

Sustained application (vicārö විචාරො) is a state present in consciousness, which has reached an object by initial application, which sustains consciousness on the object. That is to say, it has the property of sustaining coexistent consciousness and its mental properties on the object. Although both initial application and sustained application are associated with a state of consciousness at one and the same time, initial application is gross, like the sound of a bell when first rung. Sustained application is subtle, like the echo originating from the first ringing of the bell. Again, initial application is like a bird flying from the earth up the air exercising his wings, and sustained application is like the same bird who is up the air with its wings extended in its flight. Initial application is like a bee alighting on a flower and sustained application like its sucking the nutritive essence of the flower.

Sustained application is associated with the 55 classes of consciousness in which initial application is associated with and the 11 classes of the 2nd stage of Jhāna, making in all 66 classes. It is not associated with 55 classes of consciousness, namely, 10 of twice fivefold sense impressions, 11 of 3rd stage and 11 of 4th Stage of Jhāna and 23 of the 5th stage of Jhāna. This too is a factor of Jhāna. Therefore the number of classes of consciousness should be reckoned as 121.

3. DECIDING

Deciding (Adhimokkhō අධිමොක්ඛො) is a state present in consciousness, which keeps consciousness retained on the object with firm faith and decision. Its stability is like that of a post fixed on the earth several feet deep, which cannot be shaken by strong winds blowing in any direction. When there is absence of this factor in consciousness, then consciousness cannot be retained on the object and is unstable and shaky. It is only when this property is present that consciousness is stable and not shaky in respect of the object.

This property is associated with 78 classes of consciousness, leaving off 10 classes of twice five-fold sense impressions and 1 of perplexity. As this property is not a factor of the Jhānas, the number of classes reckoned here is 89.

4. EFFORT

Effort (Viriyan විරියං) is a state present in consciousness, which causes the coexistent states to make an effort in performing their functions. It is like giving support to a dilapidated house, or a commander in an army supplying necessary war materials and provisions to soldiers, which would tend to prevent them from worry and stimulate the arising of effort.

This property is obtained in 73 classes of consciousness, leaving off 16 classes, viz. 1 consciousness of five-door turning to sense impressions, 10 two five-fold sense impressions, 2 recipient consciousness and 3 investigating consciousness.

5. PLEASURABLE INTEREST.

Pleasurable interest (pīti පීති) is a state existing in consciousness, which pleases or makes the consciousness and the associated mental properties happy. For instance, when a thirsty wanderer walking in a desert meets a man and inquires where he can obtain water from, he is told that he could obtain very fine and sparkling water from a pond, which abounds in five different kinds of flowers, no sooner than he walks a certain distance along the same road. The wanderer walks faster onwards with a view to quenching his thirst as soon as possible and on seeing the pond referred to experiences a certain sensation and that state in consciousness is called pleasure. When this property arises in consciousness associated with mental properties, it is like dropping some oil on to a piece of cotton wool. Consciousness associated with mental properties is like the cotton wool, and pleasure like the oil. This pleasure is of five kinds viz. (1) a dull or slight sense of pleasure (khuddaka pīti ඛුද්දක පීති) (2) a sense of pleasure occuring moment by moment (khanika pīti ඛණික පීති) like flashes of lightning (3) a sense of oscillating pleasure through the body like the waves of the sea coming to the shore (okkantika pīti ඔක්කන්තික පීති) (4) a sense of intense pleasure amounting to thrilling emotion (ubbēga pīti උබ්බේග පීති) which enables one to take the body through the air just as a piece of cotton wool by wind without developing the 4th Jhāna (5) a sense of pleasure amounting to rapture (pharana pīti ඵරණ පීති) diffused through the body like a mountain rock rising through the ocean. When there is absence of this property in consciousness no sense of pleasure arises. It is because there is this property of pleasure in consciousness, that pleasure is experienced on perceiving objects.

This property of pleasure is associated with 51 classes of consciousness, leaving off 70 classes viz. 2 classes of immoral consciousness accompanied by grief, 55 classes accompanied by indifference, 2 classes of cognition of body and 11 classes of 4th stage of Jhāna. As this is a Jhāna factor, the number of classes is reckoned as 121.

CONATION OR DESIRE-TO-DO.

Conation, desire-to-do, (chandō ඡන්දො) is a state existing in consciousness which makes consciousness desire to take an object, like extending the arm to take an object. It is not greed, but only a desire to do. Greed and conation or desire-to-do appear as synonyms of craving. Although it is so, the property of conation or desire-to-do is only a desire to take an object, whereas greed conveys the idea of being particularly attached to the object. The property of conation is like the pieces of a pot or plate placed on a mat and greed like a sticky substance improvised for the purpose of ensnaring monkeys also so placed. When one desires to remove them from the mat, the pieces of pot or plate are easily removed, whereas the sticky substance cannot be removed. The difference between conation and greed can be seen from this illustration. Another illustration is as follows :—When a burglar breaks into a house of another and robs its possessions, an immoral consciousness rooted in greed arises. Again when he gives his belongings by way of charity, a process of thought arises, wherein a class of great moral consciousness arises accompanied by disinterestedness or freedom from greed. In a process of good or bad thought property of conation is similar and the difference between greed and conation should be understood from this illustration.

The property of conation is associated with 69 classes of consciousness, excepting 2 rooted in nescience and 18 classes of consciousness without hētus (හෙතු)

These six properties are called particular as they exist in six ways in both moral and immoral and those without hētus (හෙතු).

AÑÑA SAMĀNA

EITHER ONE OR THE OTHER

The first 7 properties common to all classes of consciousness and these six termed particular taken together are known as (Aññasamānā අඤ්ඤසමානා) being one or the other, that is to say they become moral or immoral according as they combine in moral or immoral consciousness. How can this be illustrated ? A cunning friend will join another who is performing a bad and immoral act such as killing, stealing, committing adultery and so on, and do it himself. The same person when he joins other friends doing good and moral acts such as going to a temple and offering flowers and so on, hearing the doctrine and so on, he will always likewise do the same. Therefore, these thirteen become impure and immoral when associated with the 12 classes of immoral consciousness, and pure and beautiful when associated with the beautiful moral classes of consciousness in Kāma, Rūpa and Arūpa planes and also in transcendental consciousness. When they are associated with resultant classes and ineffective classes they are neither moral nor immoral, but called abyākatā (අබ්‍යාකතා). Therefore, when contact is associated with an immoral consciousness, it is called immoral contact. In the same manner moral contact and abyākatā contact according as the classes of consciousness are moral or abyākatā. That is why it is stated in the Patisambhida Magga " ඵස්සො සියා කුසලං සියා අකුසලං සියා අව්‍යාකතං " (phassō siyā kusalañ siyā akusalañ siyā aviyākatañ). The remaining twelve properties such as feeling and so on should similarly be understood.

CLASSES OF MENTAL PROPERTIES AND THEIR DISTRIBUTION.

" Tērasaññasamānāca cuddasā kusalātathā
Sōbhanā pancavīsāti depaññāsa pavuccarē ",

තෙරසඤ්ඤ සමානාච චුද්දසා කුසලා තථා
සොභනා පඤ්චවීසාති දෙපඤ්ඤාස පවුච්චරෙ

Of the 52 mental properties 13 are neither moral nor immoral, 14 are immoral and 25 are beautiful.

> " Tēsan cittāviyuttānañ[1] yathāyōgamitō parañ
> Cittuppādēsu paccēkañ sampayōgō pavuccati ",

> තෙසං චිතතාවියුතතානං[1] යථායොගමිතොපරං
> චිතතුපපාදෙසු පචෙචකං සමපයොගො පවුචචති

The distribution of these mental properties, each in its turn, as they arise in states of consciousness, will be henceforth told, that is, in what and what classes of consciousness a particular property is associated with.

> " Satta. Sabbattha yujjanti yathā yōgan pakinnakā
> Cuddasā kusalēsvēva sōbhanēsvēva sōbhanā ",

> සතත සබබතථ යුජජනති යථා යොගං පකිණණකා
> චුදදසා කුසලෙසෙවව සොභනෙසෙවව සොභනා

7 are associated with all classes, 6 either moral or immoral according to circumstances.

14 with immoral classes of consciousness

25 with beautiful classes of consciousness

NOTE 1.

චිතතා වියුතතානං (cittā viyuttānan), that is, the mental properties (cētasikas චෙතසිකා)

HOW MENTAL PROPERTIES ARE DISTRIBUTED.

IN WHAT WAY?

In the first place, these seven universally common concomitants obtain in all the eighty-nine modes of consciousness [1].

Next, among the particular concomitants,

1. Initial application arises in 55 kinds of consciousness, to wit :—

(1) in all kinds of Kāmaloka consciousness with the exception of the twice five-fold sense impressions themselves [2].

(2) It also arises in the eleven kinds of consciousness connected with the 1st stage of Jhāna.

2. Sustained application arises in 66 kinds of consciousness, to wit: in all the above named 55 and also in the 11 kinds of consciousness connected with the 2nd stage of Jhāna.

3. Deciding arises in all kinds of consciousness with the exception of the twice five-fold sense impressions, and of consciousness accompanied by perplexity.

4. Effort arises in all kinds of consciousness with the exception, of

(1) Consciousness turning to impressions at the five doors of sense.

(2) The twice five-fold sense cognitions themselves.

(3) The act of mental reception [3].

(4) The act of investigation [4].

5. Pleasurable interest arises in all kinds of consciousness with the exception of:

(1) Consciousness accompanied by grief.

(2) Consciousness accompanied by hedonic indifference.

(3) Tactile impressions.

(4) Consciousness connected with the 4th Jhāna.

6. Conation or desire-to-do[5] arises in all kinds of consciousness with the exception of such as are not accompanied by their hētus (හෙතු) and of muddle-headed consciousness.

Taking these particular concomitants in the order described, the number of consciousness is as follows :—

" Chasaṭṭhi panca paññāsa ēkādasaca sōlasa
Sattatī vīsati chēva pakinnaka vivajjitā ",

ඡසට්ඨි පඤ්චපඤ්ඤාස එකාදසච සොළස
සත්තතී වීසතිචෙව පකිණ්ණක විවජ්ජිතා

The particular concomitants are lacking in 66, 55, 11, 16, 70 and 20 in the order given.

" Pancapaññāsa chasaṭṭhiṭṭha sattati tisattati
ēka paññāsa cēkūna sattati sapakinnakā ",

පචපඤ්ඤස ඡසට්ඨිඨසත්තති තිසත්ති
එකපඤ්ඤාස චෙකූන සත්තති සපකිණ්ණකා

The particular concomitants are associated with 55, 66, 78, 73, 51, and 69 in the order described.

NOTE 1

Cittuppāda (චිත්තුප්පාද) is literally a genesis or state of citta (consciousness) considered as constituting this or that process of mind, but the term here may be taken as representing a class, kind or mode of citta (consciousness).

NOTE 2

Twice five-fold, as accounting for the sensations being pleasurable or painful, vitakkō (විතක්කො) is absent from the initial momentary flash of visual or other sense impressions, but present in the rest of the process of sense-cognition.

NOTES 3 & 4

Sampaticcana (සම්පටිච්ඡන) and santīrana (සන්තීරණ) respectively. The act of investigation here is confined to the object presented to the mind and is therefore more or less of a passive nature.

NOTE 5

Conation or desire-to-do (chandō ඡන්දො) is akin to intention or purposive volition, and a muddle-headed and foolish man has no volition deserving the name of purposive.

CHAPTER X.

IMMORAL CONCOMITANTS

Of immoral concomitants, the four called 'mental properties common to all immoral consciousness' obtain in all the twelve classes of immoral consciousness, to wit :—

(1) dulness (mōhō මොහො)

(2) impudence (ahirikañ අහිරිකං)

(3) recklessness of consequences (anottappañ අනොත්තප්පං)

(4) distraction (uddhaccañ උද්ධච්චං)

(5) greed (lōbhō ලොභො) obtains only in the 8 kinds of consciousness rooted in appetite.

(6) error (ditthi දිට්ඨි) obtains in the 4 kinds of consciousness connected with erroneous views.

(7) conceit[1] (mānō මානො) obtains in the four kinds of consciousness, disconnected from erroneous views.

(8) Hate (dōsō දොසො), (9) envy (issā ඉස්සා), (10) selfishness (macchariyañ මච්ඡරියං) and (11) worry (kukkuccañ කුක්කුච්චං). These four obtain in the two kinds of consciousness connected with aversion.

(12) sloth (thīnañ ථිනං), and (13) torpor (middhan මිද්ධං) obtain in the five kinds of immoral consciousness which are volitional.

(14) perplexity (vicikicchā විචිකිච්ඡා) obtains only in the kind of consciousness that is accompanied by perplexity.

NOTE 1

The teachers refer to the inconstant association of conceit or pride with such views. 'Pride sometimes', that is, when a real superiority over others is the cause of self-advertisement and complacency. A similar reminder is made in the case of 'sloth and torpor' occurring in volitional consciousness. They so occur when the mind is unfit for work.

> " Sabbāpuññēsu cattārō lōbhamūlētayō katā
> dōsamūlēsu cattārō sasankhārē dvayan tathā
> vicikicchā vicikicchā cittēcāti catuddasa
> dvādasākusalēslvēva sampayujjanti pancadhā"

> සබ්බාපුඤ්ඤෙසු චත්තාරො ලොභ මූලෙ තයො කතා
> දොස මූලෙසු චත්තාරො සසංඛාරෙ වයං තථා
> විචිකිච්ඡා විචිකිච්ඡා චිත්තෙ චාති චතුද්දස
> ද්වා දසා කුසලෙසෙවව සම්පයුජ්ජන්ති පඤ්චධා.

In all demeritorious thoughts there are four, rooted in greed three, rooted in hate four, volitional two, and in consciousness conjoined with perplexity, doubt. In five ways the 14 immoral mental properties are bound to the 12 classes of immoral consciousness.

1. DULNESS OR DELUSION

Dulness or delusion (මොහො mōhō) is that state associated with consciousness which prevents it from seeing an object in reality, that is in the ultimate and highest sense. It is like looking at an object with the eyes closed or with a blue-coloured glass. When there is no dulness in consciousness, it will be only thinking of the object. When dulness is associated with consciousness, the real nature of an object cannot be seen. It is a great immoral property. It is the root of all evil. It is synonymous with Ignorance or Nescience (avijjā අවිජ්ජා) which according to dependent origination (Paticca sammuppāda පටිච්ච සමුප්පාද) is one of the two origins of the wheel of samsāra or of birth and death and not the origin of the world which has no beginning, no end. How is the real and true nature of the object not seen by dulness ? The characteristic feature of dulness is ignorance of the beginning, the end, both the beginning and end, and the law of dependent origination which teaches that all phenomena arise depending on one or more causes and that all conditioned and composite things are subject to impermanence, sorrow and devoid of a substantial entity. In the manner that absolute darkness produced by the four factors viz. a thick forest, night without any phase of the moon, midnight, thick and dark clouds, prevent one from seeing a blue or yellow object, the four factors above stated owing to dulness, will prevent one from seeing the truth of the three salient marks of impermanence, sorrow and soullessness. By reason of this dulness or ignorance, one treads a wrong path, heedless of the eightfold noble path, and consequently gets reborn in the four planes of infra-human existence.

2. IMPUDENCE

Impudence (ahirikañ අහිරිකං) is a state associated with consciousness which prevents a person from being ashamed to commit an immoral act. It is like a pig in regard to excreta. If impudence does not arise in consciousness, consciousness will not think of doing immoral deeds. When it arises in consciousness it will think of doing immoral deeds.

3. RECKLESSNESS OF CONSEQUENCES

Recklessness of consequences (anottappañ අනොත්තප්පං) is a state associated with consciousness which prevents one from being frightened to commit an immoral act. It is like fleas alighting on fire. If this property is not associated with consciousness, consciousness will be frightened to do any wrong deeds. When it is associated with consciousness it will not be frightened to do any immoral act. How is this property likened to fleas? Where there is a burning lamp, the fleas, owing to their ignorance and craving for visual objects which are attractive, alight on the lamp and get burnt. Similarly, people being under the delusion that killing, committing adultery, drinking and so on bring on happiness without any ill effects, commit bad deeds by speech, body and thought, and consequently suffer in the four planes of misery.

4. DISTRACTION

Distraction (uddhacca උද්ධච්ච) is a state associated with consciousness which makes one excited and distracted. It is like a quantity of ash disturbed by the pelting of a stone or a flag affected by strong wind. If distraction does not exist in consciousness, it will be steady and one-pointed. When distraction is associated with consciousness, it becomes excited, shaky and distracted, and never one-pointed or concentrated.

Although there are other mental properties, because this state of distraction is associated with consciousness in a very high degree, we have a class of consciousness called "upēkkha sahagata uddhacca sampayuttañ cittañ", consciousness accompanied by indifference and conjoined with distraction.

As the above four are associated always with all the 12 classes of immoral consciousness they are known as mental properties common to all classes of immoral consciousness (sabbākusala sādhārana cētasikā සබ්බාකුසල සාධාරණ චෙතසිකා).

5. GREED.

Greed (ලොභො lōbhō) is a state associated with consciousness which causes attachment to an object. It is compared to dirt in a dress, to a piece of flesh inside an unused vessel made of clay, and to a sticky substance improvised for the purpose of entrapping monkeys. In the latter case, when any eatables such as ripe fruits and so on are placed over the sticky substance, the monkey's fore limbs, hind limbs and the mouth get stuck to the sticky substance, when he makes an attempt to snatch the fruits by keeping a limb at a time, and lastly his mouth. In the same manner people who have a craving for sensuous pleasures get attracted to the five objects of sense and indulge in them excessively and unduly and are born in planes of misery. When there is no greed in consciousness it will not get attached to the object. It is only when greed is associated with consciousness that it gets attached to the object. This too is a root of immoral consciousness and a very powerful one. It is this greed that signifies the 2nd Ariyan Truth, the cause of Ill.

6. ERROR

Error (diṭṭhi දිට්ඨි) is a state associated with consciousness which makes a wrong impression of an object or an idea. It is like the appearance of a glare like water. Erroneous perceptions, views and ideas may be compared to a magic show or an unsafe path leading to a place wherein ghosts dwell. Just as a magician can transform pieces of plate, stones and so on, to silver, gold and any other substance he desires, even so by reason of erroneous perceptions, views and ideas one thinks that a sentient being possesses a substantial entity, a soul or an ātman, when there is in a being no such personal entity and that a being is only a life-flux, a continuity of material and immaterial qualities constituting matter and mind. The heinous offences of killing, drinking intoxicants and so on, are not considered as sins. He conceives that he would be, after death, born in an Everlasting Heaven or a Brahmalōka. Similarly, a person who does not wish to die but enjoy the so-called worldly pleasures of sense, with the hope of doing so for a considerable time, walks along a path leading to a place where ghosts dwell. No sooner than he reaches the place, his blood is drunk and flesh eaten by the ghosts. In the same manner, one who has erroneous perceptions, ideas and views, hoping to enjoy everlasting happiness, treads a wrong path, leading to the four planes of misery, wherein much suffering has to be experienced for a considerable period till the exhaustion of the particular kamma that conditioned rebirth there.

7. CONCEIT

Conceit (mānō මානො) is a state present in consciousness which makes one high-minded and conceited. There are nine types of conceit, namely :—

(1) one considering himself to be superior to others (seyyōhamasmi සෙය්‍යොහමස්මි).

(2) one considering himself to be an equal of others (sadisō hamasmi සදිසොහමස්මි).

(3) one considering himself to be inferior to others (heenohamasmi හීනොහමස්මි).

(4), (5), (6) same as above with reference to the past.

(7), (8) & (9) same as above with reference to the future.

The characteristic feature of conceit is a manifestation of superiority and a desire to be elevated like the hoisting of a flag.

The causes of conceit are beauty of body, riches, age and possession of good qualities, class and creed and also paying heed to one's good kamma, that is actions by body, speech and thought.

It is also classified under the three heads of (1) community by birth; (2) fortunate sense experiences occasioned by previous good kamma; (3) good qualities possessed. Conceit arises by thinking that one is descended from a royal family or belongs to a particular community. Secondly, he thinks that the enormous wealth in his possession is due to good kamma in a previous existence. Thirdly, he thinks he possesses such and such good qualities occasioned by Morality, Concentration, and Insight.

Again an inferior person may consider that he is superior to others conventionally superior to him (හීනො මානො heenō mānō). Secondly, he considers that he is an equal of others in respect of wealth, creed, class, morality and so on (sadisō mānō සදිසො මානො). Thirdly, superior people such as kings, ministers and others of a high status consider themselves to be the same as people conventionally considered as inferior (සෙය්‍යො වා පණීතො මානො seyyō or panītō mānō).

When the mental property of conceit is not associated with consciousness, consciousness will not make one think that he is superior, inferior or an equal of others. He does so only when conceit arises in consciousness.

It should be noted that error and conceit never occur together in a state of consciousness, as there is a dissimilarity between the two, just as two lions never dwell in one cave.

8. HATE

Hate (Dōsō දොසො) is a state, associated with consciousness, of anger and aversion. It causes the arising of anger in consciousness on perceiving impressions from unpleasant objects and so on, just as a snake coming out of a hiding place and attacking those that pelt stones at it, or strike it with sticks and so on. The mental property of hate lying dormant in the heart-base like a snake in a hiding place, until a person reaches the path of Never-Returning, when irritated by any of the ten causes which produce consciousness rooted in hate or aversion and accompanied by grief, suddenly arises and does harm to himself as well as to others. It may go to the extent of even killing one. Just as the rust arising in iron erodes same, even so the individual getting angry does harm to himself and ultimately destroys himself and is reborn in the four planes of misery.

9. ENVY

Envy (issā ඉස්සා) is a state of not tolerating others' success associated in consciousness. The characteristic feature of envy is frowning at others' success in life.

10. SELFISHNESS

Selfishness (macchariyañ මච්ඡරියං) is a state concealing one's possessions associated in consciousness. It is not greed. When selfishness is associated with consciousness, one does not even tolerate or wish that others should know that he is possessed of so much wealth and so on, nay, less that he would be willing to give some to others. He does not desire to share his possessions with others who are in want.

Envy arises in respect of external objects, and selfishness in respect of one's personal belongings. Envy does not tolerate others' wealth, dresses, jewels, retinue, and so on, and frowns at them, whereas selfishness, whenever occasion arises to give some of his wealth to others, never divulges the worth of a person and conceals it. These two mental properties are like two friends of hate. When either of them arises in a state of consciousness each is accompanied by hate.

11. WORRY

Worry (kukkucca කුක්කුච්ච) is a state associated with consciousness which makes one worry about the bad acts done in the past and not having done any good acts such as giving charity and so on. During one's young days having lived a life performing such bad acts as fishing, hunting, stealing, giving false evidence and so on, and in his old age associating himself with good friends such as priests and clever and learned people fit to give advice to others, if one were to give up all those bad acts and take refuge in the Triple Gem and hear the preaching of the doctrine, whilst so doing, he thinks and exclaims "Oh I shall be born in such and such a place of misery for the immoral acts done," and worries himself and repents over it. When he hears the doctrine, and the fact that those who had done good acts such as giving charity would be reborn in the six heavens and so on, comes within his knowledge, he again worries himself exclaiming "Oh what a pity, I was not able to do such and such good acts".

There is another type of individual, who worries himself about not doing good acts in the past. He is born of a very wealthy family, and inherits abundant wealth which is misused for the purpose of drinking intoxicants, leading an unchaste life, gambling and other bad acts. When at a later stage of life and when his wealth is exhausted, he has a desire to give charity but not in a position to do so and therefore he worries himself. This mental property always and invariably refers to the past and never to the present or future. It is like a slave, who has so become owing to his wrong acts. When this property exists in a very high degree, it prevents one from engaging himself in any good acts. Only Buddhas and Arahats, and other good friends can save him from his unfortunate plight and make him do good acts through the three doors during the rest of his life.

The mental properties of envy, selfishness and worry originate in the two classes of immoral consciousness accompanied by grief and rooted in hate or aversion. They arise separately and never together. In one state of consciousness only one arises, and never two or three. All the three may be absent.

12. SLOTH

Sloth (thīna ථීන) is a state retarding consciousness and making it lethargic.

13. TORPOR

Torpor (middha මිද්ධ) is a state retarding the mental properties of feeling, perception and volitional activities and making them lethargic.

Sloth and torpor arise in the five volitional classes of immoral consciousness. They always arise together and never separately. They do so only when the mind and mental properties are lethargic and not at other times.

Sloth and torpor are compared to a fire, and mind and mental properties to a feather. Just as a feather held near a fire gets shrivelled, even so the mind and mental properties associated with sloth and torpor are like the feather held near a fire. These two properties of sloth and torpor always exist together in the Pali Text. What is the reason for it? They so exist, because their functions are the same, and their contrary properties too are similar. Their function is to make the mind and mental properties lethargic and shrivelled, so to say. The state opposite or contrary to them is effort. They are categorised under the Hindrances as Thīna middha nīvarana (ථීන මිඞ නීවරණ).

Of these two, middha (මිඞ) torpor is of two varieties viz. nāma middha (නාම මිඞ) torpor of mental properties, and rūpa middha (රූප මිඞ) torpor of body. Of the two, torpor of body is not a bad kamma. The physical body which has been utilized for performing various duties during the day gets into a state of lethargy owing to weariness, just like the lotus flowers that have been affected by the rays of the sun during day getting shrivelled during night. Torpor of body is called sleep. Torpor of body is never conjoined with sloth and as in " සෙය්‍ය සුඛං මිඞ සුඛං (seyyasukhan middha sukhañ) it exists by itself. Though such be the case, there is sleep in the physical body occasioned by torpor associated with classes of immoral consciousness. How does that take place? When the five volitional classes of immoral consciousness brought on by the hindrance of sloth and torpor repeatedly arise, laziness or lethargic condition regarding the torpor of mental properties called feeling, perception and volitional activities, or the material qualities occasioned by mind, which exist in the five volitional classes of immoral consciousness, by being diffused through the physical body falls into a sleep. As the cause of that sleep is the hindrance of sloth and torpor, the commentary Atthasālini states, "පංචලායිකා නිද්ද, පච්චුපට්ඨානං (pancalāyikā niddā paccupaṭṭhānañ). This sleep or torpor of physical body is not classed under immoral states. Both the varieties of torpor of physical body arise in the worldlings and those who have entered the 1st three paths and gained fruition of the same. But in the case of Arahats, torpor of body takes place owing to weariness caused by physical exertion such as walking for begging alms and so on.

14. PERPLEXITY

Perplexity (vicikicchā විචිකිච්ඡා) is a state associated with consciousness which makes one doubt about the Buddha, Dhamma, Sangha and so on. It is like a man who has got into a junction of two roads. This only exists in that class of consciousness accompanied by indifference and conjoined with perplexity.

The characteristic feature of this property is the inability to determine the true nature of objects. It is likened to a man sleeping in a cemetery with his knees bent and back on the ground. When he gets up at night, he gets frightened thinking that both his knees are two ghosts. In like manner,one, in whom that class of consciousness associated with perplexity arises constantly, gets frightened, determining what is not bad kamma as bad, and what is not good kamma as good.

There are 16 types of doubt associated with this mental property, to wit, five regarding the past existence, five regarding the future existence and six regarding the present. With regard to the past he doubts (1) whether he ever existed (2) whether he did not exist (3) how he existed (4) as whom did he exist (5) after doing what did he depart from past existence. In respect of the future too he doubts. (1) whether he will be born after death (2) whether he will not be born again (3) how will he be born (4) as whom will he be born (5) after doing what will he be born in the future. In respect of the present he doubts (1) whether he exists (2) whether he does not exist (3) how he exists (4) as whom he is existing (5) where he, who is called an individual, came from, and (6) whither will he be going. As the class of consciousness associated with perplexity or doubt is a great immoral one almost equivalent to erroneous views, perceptions and ideas, it cannot be completely extinguished till one becomes a stream winner.

Of the immoral mental properties distraction, worry and perplexity have a great similarity to one another.

CHAPTER XI

OF MORALLY BEAUTIFUL CONCOMITANTS[1]

Now, among the concomitants called morally beautiful, in the first place, there are the nineteen mental properties common to morally beautiful consciousness. These are present in every one of the fifty-nine classes of beautiful consciousness.

Next, the three abstinences obtain always and all at once in all cases of transcendental consciousness. But in mundane [2] morally beautiful consciousness, it is only in the eight kinds of kāmalōka moral consciousness that the three are sometimes and severally apparent.

Next, reason[4] enters into combination with forty seven classes of consciousness to wit, with 12 kinds of consciousness arising in kāmalōka that are connected with knowledge and also with all the 35 kinds of sublime and of transcendental consciousness.

Next, the two illimitables spring up, sometimes and mutually exclusive, in 12 kinds of sublime[3] consciousness excluding the 5th Jhāna, in the 8 kinds of kāmalōka moral consciousness and in the 8 classes of consciousness arising in kāmalōka, which are accompanied by their respective hētus (හේතු) and which are ineffective, making up altogether 28 classes.

Some teachers, however, say, that 'pity' and 'appreciation' are not in such consciousness as is accompanied by hedonic indifference.

NOTE 1

Sōbhanā (සෝභනා) is, literally, beautiful. It signifies aesthetic consciousness with mirth.

NOTE 2

Lōkiya (ලෞකික) means of the three lōkas or spheres of existence. It is the opposite of lōkuttara (ලොකුත්තර) transcendental.

NOTE 3

Mahaggata cittēsu (මහග්ගත චිත්තෙසු). The Ceylon Commentaries explain this term as meaning those classes of consciousness that have grown great or become exalted or sublime. because of the absence of hindrances, etc. (vinīvaranāditāya mahattañ gatāni විනීවරණාදිතාය මහත්තං ගතානි), or by reason of the excellent Jhānas (Mahantēhi Jhāyēehi gatāni මහන්තෙහි ඣායීහි ගතානි). According to the Venerable Buddhaghosa it is so termed because of the ability to resist vice, produces abundance of good result of wide extension, of attainment to a high pitch of volition, energy, thought, wisdom.

NOTE 4

පඤ්ඤා (paññā) the factor here combining with the forty seven is, according to circumstances, knowledge intellect, understanding, insight, right view or wisdom factor (bojjhanga බොජ්ඣඞ්ග).

CONCOMITANTS IN FOUR GROUPS

" Ekūnaveesatī dhammā Jāyantēkūna saṭṭhisu
tayō sōlasa cittēsu aṭṭhaveesati yan dvayan."

එකූනවීසතිධම්මා ජායන්තෙකූනසට්ඨිසු
තයො සොළස චිත්තෙසු අට්ඨවීසතියං ද්වයං

19 mental concomitants arise in 59 classes of consciousness, 3 in 16 classes and 2 in 28 classes.

" Paññāpakāsitā satta cattālisa vidhēsupi
sampayuttā catuddhēvan sobhanēsvēva sōbhanā "

පඤ්ඤාපකාසිතා සත්ත චත්තාලීසවිධෙසුපි
සම්පයුත්තා චතුධෙවං සොභනෙසෙවව සොභනා

Reason is said to arise in 47 classes. Therefore the beautiful concomitants arise in beautiful classes of consciousness in four groups.

CONCOMITANTS AS ACCIDENTAL AND AS ESSENTIAL

" Issāmacchēra kukkuccā viratī karunādayō
nānā kadāci mānōca thīnamiddhan tathā sahā

" Yathā vuttānusārēna sēsā niyatayōginō
sangahanca pavakkhāmi tēsandāni yathārahan "

ඉස්සා මච්ඡෙර කුක්කුච්චා විරතී කරුණාදයො
නානාකදාචි මානොච ථීනමිද්ධං තථා සහ
යථා වුත්තානුසාරෙන සෙසා නියතයොගිනො
සඞ්ගහංච පවක්ඛාමි තෙසන්දානි යථාරහං

envy, selfishness and worry, the three abstinences, pity and appreciation, conceit, sloth and torpor appear sometimes and severally. If these are remembered, the rest are all necessary adjuncts which always appear in consciousness. Now all these concomitants I'll try to fit into a synthesis where they permit.

SYNTHESIS OF CONCOMITANTS

" Chattingsānuttarē dhammā pancatinsa mahaggatē
aṭṭhatinsāpi labbhanti kāmāvacara sōbhanē
Sattaveesattyapuññamhi dvādasā hētukētica
yathā sambhavayogēna pancadhā tattha sangaho "

ඡත්තිංසානුත්තරෙ ධම්මා පඤ්චතිංස මහග්ගතෙ
අට්ඨතිංසාපි ලබ්භන්ති කාමාවචර සොභනෙ
සත්තවීසත්‍ය පුඤ්ඤම්හි ද්වාදසාහෙතුකෙතිච
යථා සම්භවයොගෙන පඤ්චධාතත්ථ සඞ්ගහො

Into our highest thoughts come thirty six, and thirty five into thoughts sublime, and into Kāmalōka consciousness of loveliness and beauty thirty eight. In thoughts demeritorious twenty seven, and twelve in thoughts that rise without hētu. Five-fold the synthesis of adjuncts stands duly assorted as they come to pass. How is it so?

SYNTHESIS IN TRANSCENDENTAL CONSCIOUSNESS

First of all, in transcendental consciousness there are 36 concomitant states which enter into combination with any one of the eight classes of consciousness arising in the 1st Jhāna, namely, the 13 unmoral concomitants and 23 beautiful concomitants omitting only the two illimitables. The two illimitables are excluded because their object which is satta paññatti (සත්ත පඤ්ඤත්ති) "the concept mankind" is totally different from that of transcendental consciousness namely Nibbāna.

Similarly, 35 concomitant states, initial application being now excluded, enter into combination with any one of the eight classes of consciousness arising in the 2nd Jhāna.

Similarly, 34 concomitant states, initial application and sustained application being now excluded, enter into combination with any one of the eight classes of consciousness arising in the 3rd Jhāna. Similarly, 33 concomitant states, initial application, sustained application and pleasurable interest being now excluded, enter into combination with anyone of the eight classes arising in the 4th Jhāna. And 33 concomitant states, hedonic indifference replacing pleasure, enter into combination with any one of the eight classes of consciousness arising in the 5th Jhāna.

Thus, under all circumstances there is only a five-fold synthesis of concomitants with the eight kinds of transcendental consciousness corresponding to the five stages of Jhāna.

> "Chattinsa pancatinsātha catuttinsa yathākkaman
> tettinsaddvaya miccēvan pancadhānuttarē ṭhitā"
>
> ඡත්තිංස පංචතිංසාථ චතුත්තිංස යථාක්කමං
> තෙත්තිංසද්වය මිච්චෙවං පංචධානුත්තරෙඨිතා

Five-fold the synthesis that stands in highest plane of thought from thirty six to thirty three, the last taken twice is taught.

SYNTHESIS IN SUBLIME CONSCIOUSNESS

Next, in sublime consciousness, there are 35 factors which enter into combination with anyone of those three[1] classes of consciousness that belong to the 1st stage of Jhāna, namely, 13 unmoral concomitants and 22 morally beautiful concomitants, the three "Abstinences" being excluded.[2] Here be it noted that "pity" and "appreciation" combine severally only.

Again the same concomitants, with the exception of initial application, enter into combination with any one of the three classes of consciousness that belong to the 2nd stage of Jhāna and also to the 3rd and 4th stages dropping in succession application, both initial and sustained, at the 3rd stage, and these two and pleasurable interest at the fourth stage.

But in the 15 classes of consciousness that belong to the 5th stage of Jhāna the two illimitables do not obtain.

Thus reckoning every possible way, the combinations of concomitants, with the 27 kinds of sublime consciousness by way of five-fold Jhāna may be summarized under five heads.

Note 1

Moral, resultant and ineffective consciousness.

Note 2

Because they do not bear on the object of Jhāna practice and they are totally different in function from Jhāna. The function of the three "Abstinences" is to purify act and word either temporarily or permanently, whilst the function of Jhāna is to purify the mind of one who has already had his act and word purified.

" Pancatinsa catuttinsa tettinsaca yathākkaman
dvattinsa cēvatinsēti pancadhāva mahaggatē "

පඤ්චතිංස චතුත්තිංස තෙත්තිංසච යථාක්කමං
ද්වත්තිංස චෙවතිංසෙති පඤ්චධාව මහග්ගතෙ

Five-fold are the groups in sublime consciousness, namely, 35, 34, 33, 32 and 30.

SYNTHESIS OF MORALLY BEAUTIFUL CONSCIOUSNESS IN KĀMALŌKA

Next in morally beautiful consciousness in Kāmalōka, in the first place, there are 38 states, which enter into combination in any of the first two classes of moral consciousness, namely, automatic and the volitional, to wit, the 13 unmoral concomitants and the 25 morally beautiful concomitants.

Here it should be noted that the two 'Illimitables' and the three 'Abstinences' combine separately.

Similarly these 38 enter into combination in any one of the second two, 'knowledge' only being excluded; in any one of the third two, 'Knowledge' being included, but 'pleasurable interest' being excluded; and in any one of the fourth two, both 'Knowledge' and 'pleasurable interest' being excluded.

Again taking the eight kinds of Kāmalōka ineffective consciousness and excluding the three 'Abstinences', those 38 now 35 concomitant states are to be reckoned as similarly combining in four different ways, in four pairs of ineffective classes of consciousness.

And again, taking the eight kinds of Kāmalōka resultant consciousness and excluding both the two 'Illimitables' and the three 'Abstinences', those 38 now 33 concomitant states are to be reckoned as similarly combining in four different ways in four pairs of resultant kinds of consciousness.

Thus reckoning every possible way the combinations of morally beautiful concomitants in pairs with the 24 morally beautiful classes of Kāmalōka consciousness may be summarized under twelve heads.

> "Aṭṭhatinsa sattatinsadvayan chattinsakan subhē
> pancatinsa catuttinsadvayan tettinsakan kriyē
>
> "Tettinsapākē dvattinsadveyē kattinsa kan bhavē
> sahētukāmāvacarȧ puññapāka kriyāmanē"

> අට්ඨතිංස සත්තතිංසවයං ඡත්තිංසකං සුභෙ
> පංචතිංස චතුත්තිංසවයං තෙත්තිංසකං ක්‍රියෙ
>
> තෙත්තිංස පාකෙවත්තිං සවෙයෙකත්තිංසංකං භවෙ
> සහෙතුකාමාවචර පුඤ්ඤපාක ක්‍රියාමනෙ

In Kāmalōka classes of consciousness bound to hētus (හෙතු) there are. 38, 37, 37 and 36 concomitants in moral classes; 35, 34, 34 and 33 in ineffective classes, and 33, 32, 32, and 31 in resultant classes.

"Navijjantettha virati kriyāsuca mahaggatē
Anuttarē appamaññā kāmapākē dvayan tathā
"Anuttarē jhānadhammā appamaññāca majjhimē
virati ñāna pīti ca parittēsu visēsaka"

න විජ්ජන්තෙත්ථ විරති ක්‍රියාසුච මහග්ගතෙ
අනුත්තරෙ අප්පමඤ්ඤා කාමපාකෙ ද්වයං තථා
අනුත්තරෙ ඣානධම්මා අප්පමඤ්ඤා ච මජ්ඣිමෙ
විරති ඤාණපීති ච පරිත්තෙසු විසෙසකා

The three 'Abstinences' never arise in ineffective and sublime thoughts, nor do the Illimitables in transcendental thought. And in resultant classes both the 'Abstinences' and 'Illimitables' never arise.

In transcendental consciousness the Jhāna stages show a distinction, and in sublime the 'Illimitables' and in lower planes the three 'Abstinences', knowledge and pleasurable interest show a distinction.

SYNTHESIS OF IMMORAL CONCOMITANTS

Now in immoral consciousness, in the first place, there are nineteen concomitant states which enter into combination with anyone of the first automatic class in the eight kinds of consciousness called appetitives or rooted in greed, namely, the 13 unmoral concomitants and the 4 common immoral concomitants, making seventeen, to which add greed and error. In like manner with the second automatic class, the same seventeen concomitants combine, together with greed and conceit. In like manner with the third automatic class, the same 17 concomitants combine with the exception of pleasurable interest, but together with greed and error, giving 18 in all.

In like manner with the fourth automatic class, omitting pleasurable interest, but adding greed and conceit. But with the fifth automatic class which is connected with aversion, to the 17 foregoing concomitants add hate, envy, selfishness and worry and from them omit pleasurable interest, thus making 20 concomitants combining with that fifth class.

But of these four envy, selfishness and worry can only combine separately. In like manner with the five corresponding volitional classes of the twelve kinds of immoral cognition, the foregoing combinations of concomitants obtain, with this difference that sloth and torpor must be included.

Excluding desire-to-do and pleasurable interest, eleven unmoral and the four common immoral concomitants, fifteen states in all, are associated with that class of consciousness which is accompanied by distraction.

In like manner with that class of consciousness accompanied by perplexity, 15 concomitants deprived of the element of 'deciding' but accompanied by perplexity combine well.

Thus, all being reckoned, there is a seven-fold synthesis of concomitants numerically considered, combining with the 12 kinds of immoral consciousness.

> " Ekūnaveesaṭṭhārasa veesēkaveesa veesaṭi
> dvēveesa pannarasēti sattadhā kusalē ṭhitā
>
> " Sādhāranāca cattārō samānāca dasāparē
> cuddasētē pavuccanti sabbākusala yōginō "

එකූනවීසට්ඨාරස. විසෙකා වීසවීසති
වෙවීස පණ්ණරසෙති සත්තධාකුසලෙ ඨිතා

සාධාරණාච චත්තාරො සමානාච දසාපරෙ
චුද්දසෙතෙ පවුච්චන්ති සබ්බාකුසලයොගිනො

With evil thoughts the immoral concomitants stand under 7 groups namely, 19, 18, 20, 21, 20, 22 and 15. With every immoral thought 14 mental concomitants always arise viz the four common to all classes of immoral consciousness and ten besides, that is with the exception of desire-to-do, pleasurable interest and deciding from the 13 unmoral concomitants.

SYNTHESIS OF UNMORAL MENTAL CONCOMITANTS

Lastly, in consciousness not accompanied by hētus (හෙතු), there are 12 of the 13 unmoral concomitants, desire-to-do being excluded, which enter into combination, in the consciousness of aesthetic pleasure.

They combine also in the consciousness of determining[1], pleasurable interest being excluded as well as desire-to-do, and again with the consciousness of investigation with pleasure and effort being excluded as well as desire-to-do.

They combine also with the triple faculty of apprehension[2] and with the dual process[3] of rebirth consciousness, which is not accompanied by its hētus. Here desire-to-do, pleasurable interest and effort are excluded.

Lastly, they combine with the twice five groups of sense-cognitions. Here, however, all the 'particular' concomitants must be excluded.

Thus, all being reckoned, the synthesis of concomitants numerically considered combining with the 18 classes of consciousness not accompanied by their hētus (හෙතු) consists of 4 groups.

NOTE 1

Vottappana (වොතතපපන) fixing, assigning impressions, the stage before apperception.

NOTE 2

The triple faculty of apprehension (manodhātu මනොධාතු) comprises the mind 'turning towards' stimuli (pancadvārāvajjana පඤ්චද්වාරාවජ්ජන) and the two recipient elements (sampaṭicchana සම්පටිච්ඡන) capable of taking part only in a presentative cognition with any one of the five sensibles as their object, and never in a representative.

NOTE 3

The two classes of rebirth consciousness are the two classes of consciousness called upēkkhā sahagata santirana (උපෙක්ඛා සහගත සන්තීරණ) investigating consciousness with indifference, which is capable of performing five different functions. It may be questioned as to why five different designations are not given corresponding to each function. The reply is that one class of consciousness functions on different occasions in five ways, as an individual can be at once a poet, a philosopher, a politician, a musician, and a philanthropist.

" Dvādasēkādasadasa sattacāti cattubbidho
aṭṭhārasāhētukēsu cittuppādēsu sangaho

" ahētukēsu sabbattha sattasēsa yathārahan
iti vitthāratō vuttā tettinsavidha sangahā

" itthan cittāviyuttānan sampayōganca sangahan
ñatvabhēdan yathāyōgan cittēna samamuddisēti "

ද්වාදසෙකාදසදස සතත චාති චතුබ්බිධො
අටඨාරස අහෙතුකෙසු චිතතුපපාදෙසු සංගහො

අහෙතුකෙසු සබබතථ සතත සෙසා යථාරහං
ඉති විතථාරතො වුතතා තෙතතිංසවිධ සඞගහා

ඉතථං චිතතාවියුතතානං සමපයොගංච සංගහං
ඤතවා භෙදං යථායොගං චිතෙතන සමමුද්දිසෙති

The mental concomitants combining with the 18 classes of consciousness unaccompanied by hētus (හෙතු) are classed under 4 groups of 12, 11, 10 and 10. 7 are common to all the 18 classes and the remaining combine according to circumstances.

Now in detail you see the mental concomitants in summaries of 33 namely 5—5—12—7—4=33. Thus we have come to know the summary and methods of the mind's concomitants. Hence the manner in which the concomitants are associated with consciousness can be hereafter explained.

25 Morally Beautiful concomitants.

CONFIDENCE

1. Confidence (saddhā සද්ධා) is a state associated with consciousness which makes the other mental concomitants have confidence in the Buddha, Dhamma and Sangha. There are two characteristic features in it, namely, sampasādana (සම්පසාදන) and Sampakkhandana (සම්පක්ඛන්දන). The first is like the mānikkyaratna (මාණික්‍ය රතන) of a chakkavatti king, which has the property of making any impure and dirty water quite clear, sparkling, wholesome and pure by removing all the impurities such as mud, dirt and any organic material. Just as this mānikkyaratna when inserted in water, makes it clear, sparkling, wholesome, absolutely pure and fit for

consumption, even so when there is confidence in the Buddha Dhamma and Sangha the torments and defilements lying dormant and associated with one's consciousness temporarily disappear and the consciousness becomes pure and sparkling. The second feature sampakkhandana (සම්පක්ඛන්දන) destroys immoral states in consciousness and causes the performance of morally beautiful acts. This is illustrated by the way in which a brave and daring man at the risk of his life gets into a stream of water infested with dangerous animals such as crocodiles and so on and kills them with a sword, thus enabling those who feared to cross the stream, to do so without any fear.

Good moral acts such as charity and so on are done by people only when there is confidence. When there is no confidence, no good act can be done. The controlling power of confidence and the force of confidence are so called because of the presence of confidence in them. It is present in every one of the 59 classes of beautiful consciousness.

MINDFULNESS

2. Mindfulness (Sati සති) is a state associated with consciousness which makes the mental concomitants think of the attributes of the Buddha, Dhamma and Sangha, and also contemplate mind and body as possessing the three salient features of impermanence, sorrow and soul-lessness. It is like the treasurer of a Chakkavatti King. He makes a statement of accounts in respect of the King's wealth in gold, silver, jewels and so on and also his liabilities in respect of salaries and so on to be paid to his servants. The king by reason of his being attached to sensuous pleasures to be derived from the five doors of sense completely forgets his assets and liabilities. The Treasurer waits for a suitable occasion and places at his disposal statement of accounts and reminds that such and such good actions should be done in the future too by way of giving charity. Then the King becomes mindful of his possessions, of the good acts performed and of what good actions he should perform in the future and becomes greatly pleased and happy. After the departure of the Treasurer, the King again falling a victim to sense desires forgets everything that was brought before his mind's eye. Again and again the Treasurer continues to remind the King when, he becomes mindful. Similarly, the ordinary

individual owing to craving for sense desires originating from greed, hate and nescience, becomes unmindful of the good acts he should do, and completely forgets to contemplate mind and body as transient, sorrow and devoid of a substantial entity. But on the appearance of mindfulness in his consciousness he will contemplate the attributes of the Buddha, Dhamma, Sangha and the impermanent nature of mind and body and thereby accumulate much merit. This type of mindfulness is called apilāpana sati (අපිලාපන සති).

There is another type of mindfulness called upagganhana sati (උපග්ගණ්හන සති). Its characteristic is to prevent forgetfulness of objects and reproduce any matter that has been learnt and digested. It is compared to a stone inscription which cannot be easily deleted. It is mindfulness of arts and sciences studied in school days at a later stage in life. This type of mindfulness enables one to even remember incidents and events that occured in his past births, if he is capable of developing the 5th stage of Jhāna. The reminiscence of past births for innumerable kappas or aeons by the Buddhas. Pacceka Buddhas and Arahats (The latter only for a limited number) is solely done by this characteristic of the mental property of mindfulness.

Again, mindfulness is compared to a care-taker of a house with six doors of entrance. The caretaker prevents the entrance of rogues into the house through any of the doors. Similarly, the mindfulness called the caretaker prevents the torments and defilements called the rogues gaining entrance through the six sensory organs called the doors into the mind and body called the house.

It is this mental property that occurs in some of the factors pertaining to enlightenment such as satipaṭṭhāna (සතිපට්ඨාන) mindfulness of body, satindriya (සතින්ද්‍රිය) faculty of mindfulness, satibala (සති බල) force of mindfulness, satisambojjhanga (සති සම්බොජ්ඣඞ්ග) the wisdom factor of mindfulness and sammāsati (සම්මා සති) right mindfulness.

PRUDENCE

3. Prudence (හිරි) is a state associated with consciousness which causes shame to do immoral acts through the body and so on. It is like a respectable young lady. In recognition of

one's personality, one is ashamed to do immoral acts. It has the feature of self-respect, and therefore one does not commit evil. It is like a cold rod of iron stained with excreta. Although touching the rod of iron gives a pleasant sensation, one fears to touch the rod owing to the excreta on it. It is also compared to a young lady of a respectable family. When she encounters a man, she considers herself to be much superior to him. She thinks of her geneology and states that no woman in her ancestry ever misbehaved. Therefore, if I were to do an immoral act the public will put me into an indelible shame and it will blemish my ancestry. Considering all these facts about herself she refrains from committing an immoral act.

This mental property arises from four causes (1) birth in a particular caste or community (2) age (3) dexterity and (4) great learning. Considering one's heritage one refrains from committing evil like fishing, hunting and drinking intoxicating liquor and so on. He considers that these are the immoral acts of people of low birth. Another thinks that a person of my age should not kill nor drink intoxicants and refrains from them. Another thinks that he must maintain himself by engaging himself in such occupations as agriculture, trade and so on. These immoral acts are usually committed by the unemployed owing to their laziness, and considering his dexterity he refrains from them.

Another thinks that these immoral acts are committed by the uneducated foolish people, and a person like himself who has had a liberal education in arts, sciences etc. should not demean himself by doing these immoral acts and refrains from them.

DISCRETION

4. Discretion (ottappa ඔත්තප්ප) is a state associated with consciousness which frightens one from doing immoral acts. He fears he would be reborn in the four planes of misery, if he were to commit evil and accordingly refrains from doing them in recognition of the external objects. He refrains from evil fearing public disgrace. This property is compared to a red hot iron rod. One does not hold it, owing to the fear of his hand being burnt. Again, it is compared to a woman who observes the Precepts. When a man approaches a woman observing the Precepts, she refrains from doing anything immoral in consideration of the Precepts, which she is frightened to violate.

This mental property arises from four causes viz (1) Morality (2) District (3) Reason or knowledge and (4) the state of being a Bhikkhu.

When occasion arises to do an immoral act, he fears that he would be disgraced by the virtuous Bhikkhus and the laity and also the Devas and Brahmas and refrains from it. Another through the fear of the district, wherein prevails the Buddha Dhamma and Sangha, refrains from committing evil. He fears the people in the district who pay reverence to the Triple Gem and are virtuous. Another refrains from evil owing to the fear he has for the learned and educated class of people, for, if he were to do so, he would be disgraced by them. Another refrains from committing evil in consideration of the state of a Bhikkhu, as it would be most unbecoming for a Bhikkhu to do so.

These two mental properties of Prudence and Discretion are the two main causes of origination of morally beautiful classes of consciousness. They are also called Dēva Dhammā (දෙව ධම්මා) and Loka pālaka dhammā (ලෝක පාලක ධම්මා), states of the Devas and states maintaining the world.

DISINTERESTEDNESS

5. Disinterestedness (Alōbha අලෝභ) is a state associated with consciousness which keeps it detached from objects and takes no interest in them. It is compared to an Arahat in whom there is extinction of āsavas (desires, torments, defilements etc.) How so ? When an Arahat dwelling in a monastery provided by a house-holder who gives robes, meals, bedding and medicines indispensable for sustenance, leaves same, he does so without taking any interest in the monastery or its belongings. Because there is the presence of lack of interest or detachment in disinterestedness it is compared to an Arahat. Again, just as water poured over a flower drops down without a drop remaining intact on the petals, even so the mental concomitant of disinterestedness does not get attached to any object. Again, just as a person who has fallen into a pit containing excreta will without delay make an effort to purify himself, even so will this property of disinterestedness make an effort to give by way of charity objects of sense experience through the five-doors of a person born in Kāmalōka.

This is a great moral action, and a root of moral consciousness.

AMITY

6. Amity (අදොස adōsa) is a state associated with consciousness which prevents it from showing a hate or aversion to an object. How could this be illustrated? Just as a friend who has been away from the island to a remote place for a considerable period is given a warm reception by his friends and relations on his return and congratulations offered on his achievement of success, even so does the mental property of amity show benevolence and goodwill to all beings.

This is a great moral act and a root of moral consciousness. It is mettā (මෙත්තා) benevolence or goodwill, the first of the four Brahamavihāras. Of the two, disinterestedness and amity, disinterestedness is the opposite of selfishness and greed and amity of aversion and hate. Charity is caused by disinterestedness and morality by amity. As greed shrouds faults, by disinterestedness existing faults are seen as faults. As aversion and hate shroud or delete the good qualities, by amity the existing good qualities are seen as such. By disinterestedness sorrow occasioned by parting with the dear and near disappears and by amity sorrow occasioned by associating with undesirable beings disappears. Further, by disinterestedness sorrow occasioned by birth disappears and by amity that brought on by decay.

BALANCE OF MIND.

7. Balance of mind or equanimity (tatramajjhattatā තත්‍රමජ්ඣත්තතා) is a state associated with consciousness which keeps the other associated mental concomitants well balanced in respect of an object. It is like the driver of a chariot with a pair of horses. He neither holds the reins too tight nor too loose and holds them well balanced and sees that the pair runs alike and symmetrically.

It is also called upēkkhā (උපෙක්ඛා) that is hedonic indifference and not the vēdanā upēkkhā (වෙදනා උපෙක්ඛා) that is the indifferent feeling neither pleasant nor unpleasant.

8. COMPOSURE OF MENTAL PROPERTIES

Composure of mental properties (Kāya passaddhi කාය පස්සද්ධි). Here kāya means the three aggregates of feeling, perception and volitional activities or the mental concomitants. Passaddhi means composure. Hence composure of mental properties is kāya passaddhi (කාය පස්සද්ධි). This property is opposite to that of distraction which causes restlessness of mental properties. Therefore the characteristic feature of this property is a composure of mental properties.

9. COMPOSURE OF MIND

Composure of mind (citta passaddhi චිත්ත පස්සද්ධි). Citta is the aggregate of consciousness or mind. Composure of mind is citta passaddhi (චිත්ත පස්සද්ධි). The characteristic feature of this property is composure of mind and is opposite to that of distraction which causes restlessness of mind.

How could this be illustrated? It is like the disappearance of weariness of the body when one sits under a huge tree, which is shady, after a prolonged journey in hot sun. In this illustration composure of mind and mental properties is like the disappearance of weariness and distraction is like the hot sun. In moral consciousness belonging to Kāmalōka the composure of mind and mental concomitants conjointly prevents the arising of distraction or restlessness. Nevertheless, in classes of transcendental consciousness only one exists as the wisdom factor of serenity (පස්සද්ධි සම්බොජ්ඣඞ්ග passaddhi sambojjhanga).

10. BUOYANCY OF MIND AND MENTAL PROPERTIES

Buoyancy of mental properties (Kāya lahutā කාය ලහුතා). 11. Buoyancy of mind (citta lahutā චිත්ත ලහුතා) kāya and citta are the same as stated before. Kāya lahutā is lightness of mental properties and citta lahutā is lightness of mind. Their characteristic feature is to cause the disappearance of heaviness of mind and mental concomitants which are occasioned by sloth and torpor. It is like the relief obtained by putting down a heavy load carried on one's back after walking a considerable distance. These two are the opposite of the hindrance of sloth and torpor.

12. PLIANCY OF MIND AND MENTAL PROPERTIES

Pliancy of mental properties (kāya mudutā කාය මුදුතා). 13. Pliancy of mind (citta mudutā චිත්ත මුදුතා) Their characteristic feature is to cause the hardness of mental properties and mind occasioned by erroneous views and conceit supple and pliant. It is like two people engaged for the purpose of making a thick and hard hide of an ox or sheep supple and pliant. They do so by pouring oil, water and other materials on the hide and with much pressure from their limbs they affect a pliancy of the hide. Similarly the pliancy of mind and mental properties conjointly remove the hardness of mind and mental properties due to erroneous views and conceit. These two are the opposites of erroneous views and conceit.

14. FITNESS OF WORK OF MENTAL PROPERTIES

Fitness of work of mental properties (kāya kammaññatā කාය කම්මඤ්ඤතා) 15. fitness of work of mind (citta kammaññatā චිත්ත කම්මඤ්ඤතා). Their characteristic feature is to cause the disappearance of the inert and inactive condition of the mental properties regarding the performance of moral deeds. They are the opposites of the hindrance of 'sense desires'. Just as a piece of gold adulterated with brass and copper is unfit for dissolution till it is heated and thereafter it can be utilized for making earrings or rings, even so the hindrance of 'sense desires' when heated by these two properties are fit and capable of doing good moral deeds such as charity and so on.

16. PROFICIENCY OF MENTAL PROPERTIES AND MIND

Proficiency of mental properties (kāya pāguññatā කාය පාගුඤ්ඤතා).

17. Proficiency of mind (citta pāguññatā චිත්ත පාගුඤ්ඤතා). Their characteristic feature is to remove or relieve the diseased condition of mental properties and the mind. It is like either relieving or curing a disease of a person on the verge of death. Similarly, these two properties remove the lack of confidence, and lack of mindfulness which are dangerous qualities and make him proficient in respect of good moral acts.

18. RECTITUDE OF MENTAL PROPERTIES AND MIND

Rectitude of mental properties (kāyujjukatā කායුජ්ජුකතා): 19. Rectitude of mind (cittujjukatā චිත්තුජ්ජුකතා). Their characteristic feature is to cause the disappearance of crookedness of mind and its mental concomitants. How can this be illustrated? Just as a veddah is unable to use a crooked arrow to his contentment and satisfaction, and can only do so after rectifying its crookedness, even so, when the crookedness called the twelve immoral classes of consciousness is rectified by the veddah called the rectitude of mind and mental concomitants, could the arrow called the morally beautiful classes of consciousness be made to reach any spot the veddah desires. These two properties are the opposites of crookedness and cunningness.

It would have been seen that the last 12 mental concomitants were given in pairs, as they had the power to inhibit their opposite characteristics. The remaining nine have no such properties.

Just as the aggregate of material qualities called the body falls into sleep by the diffusion of material qualities originating from mind conquered by the hindrance of sloth and torpor, even so does the physical body become composed, light, pliant, fit for work and so on by reason of the diffusion throughout the body of material qualities originating from the mind associated with these six pairs.

These nineteen mental concomitants are common to all classes of morally beautiful consciousness viz 59.

CHAPTER XIII

THE THREE ABSTINENCES

1. Right speech (sammā vācā සම්මා වාචා) is good and proper speech, that is to say, refraining from bad and improper speech (micchā vācā මිච්ඡා වාචා). Right speech is refraining from speaking an untruth, carrying tales, the use of harsh and abusive language, indulgence in meaningless and unprofitable conversations.

2. Right action (sammā kammantō සම්මා කම්මන්තො) is good and proper bodily actions, that is to say, refraining from bad and improper actions (micchā kammantō මිච්ඡා කම්මන්තො). Right action is refraining from killing, stealing and committing adultery.

3. Right livelihood (sammājeevo සම්මාජීවො) is the correct and proper livelihood as opposed to wrong and improper means of livelihood (micchājeevo මිච්ඡාජීවො). Right livelihood is for the sake of livelihood abstaining from speaking an untruth, carrying tales, the use of harsh and abusive language, indulgence in meaningless and unprofitable talks, killing, stealing and being unchaste. Although only seven are mentioned here, there are many others such as false pretensions, partiality, flattery and many other improper attitudes adopted to curry favour and so on that should be refrained from for the purpose of right livelihood. For details of wrong livelihood vide Visuddhi Magga, or Path of Purity.

The three abstinences are obtained in three ways viz (1) when occasion arises (2) by taking the Precepts and (3) by complete extinction. Without taking the precepts or without complete extinction, when one refrains from speaking an untruth and so on as occasion arises, it is called abstinence when occasion arises (sampatta virati සම්පත්ත විරති). When one refrains from them in the future by reason of the precepts taken, it is called abstinence by taking the precepts (samādāna virati සමාදාන විරති). It is known as abstinence from complete extinction (samucchēda virati සමුච්ඡේද විරති), when they arise in classes of transcendental consciousness such as stream-attainment.

Therefore, the three abstinences are obtained in classes of transcendental consciousness always and all the three at one and the same time, whereas among the worldly classes of consciousness they exist only in the eight classes of moral consciousness in kāmaloka separately and one at a time as opportunity affords. When one abstains from speaking an untruth and so on, then right speech is associated with the eight classes of moral consciousness, but not right action and right livelihood. At the time one abstains from improper and wrong bodily actions such as killing and so on, right action becomes associated and not right speech and right livelihood. When one abstains from wrong means of living by speaking an untruth and so on, right livelihood becomes associated and not the right speech and right action.

It is these three abstinences that are mostly known as morality (sīla සීල). Although the mental properties called the three abstinences are morally beautiful, they do not arise in sublime classes of consciousness (Mahaggata මහග්ගත) viz those of rūpalōka and arūpalōka.

THE ILLIMITABLES

1. Pity (karunā කරුණා) is a state associated with consciousness which moves one's mind when another is seen suffering. Its characteristic feature is the desire to relieve sufferings not only of mankind but of all sentient beings. It is immaterial and not of any concern whether the suffering could be relieved or not. The object for pity is all sentient beings.

2. Appreciation (muditā මුදිතා) is sympathetic joy, or a state of congratulatory or benevolent attitude associated with consciousness when pleasure and happiness are seen to be enjoyed by others. Its characteristic feature is to appreciate and feel joyful over others' success and fortune. For appreciation the object is happy and fortunate beings. These two are called " the illimitables " as they have for their object all living beings which are illimitable.

There are four illimitables viz amity, pity, appreciation and equanimity. Amity and equanimity have been previously described as they are common to all classes of morally beautiful consciousness.

REASON

Paññā (පඤ්ඤා) reason is insight, clear understanding or knowledge of all things conditioned and composite as possessing the three salient features of impermanence, sorrow and absence of a soul or substantial entity. This is a very strong and great moral thought. It is a root of moral classes of consciousness.

The difference in (Saññā සඤ්ඤා) perception, (viññāna විඤ්ඤාණ) cognition and (paññā පඤ්ඤා) insight should be noted here. Perception only receives an impression of an object such as blue or green and so on, but does not realise its characteristic features, like a small child possessing knowledge in respect of a sovereign. Cognition perceives the impression and realises its characteristics, like a villager possessing knowledge in respect of a sovereign. Insight perceives the impression, realises its characteristics, and contemplates the object under the three salient features of transiency and so on or that the object is composed of nothing more than the four great essentials and so on. It is like a gold smith knowing the amount of gold in the sovereign and what amount of alloy there is in it, how it can be dissolved and utilized for making rings, earrings and so on.

It is this insight that is described under the factors pertaining to Enlightenment such as Iddhi—Potency of Investigation (වීමංසිද්ධිපාද veemansiddhipāda), faculty of reason (පඤ්ඤින්ද්‍රියං paññindriyan), the force of reason (පඤ්ඤා බලං paññā balan), enlightenment factor of searching the truth (ධම්මවිචය සම්බොජ්ඣඞ්ගං dhamma vicaya sambojjhangan) and right views (සම්මා දිට්ඨි sammā diṭṭhi). In the highest possible degree it is omniscient.

This faculty of reason has the power of controlling all other mental concomitants associated with the state of consciousness of any of the Paths or their fruition. It may be compared to a sharp piercing arrow that is capable of piercing a thick tree. Just as a clever man can send a sharp piercing arrow right through a thick tree, even so could this faculty of reason realise all phenomena that are existent in the three worlds as such and such in reality and in the ultimate and highest sense. Again, just as any existing object in darkness could only be seen by lighting a lamp, so could the faculty of reason realise the three salient features of all phenomena, analyse mind and body with reference to their features, essential properties, resulting phenomena and proximate causes, comprehend the law of dependent origination and so on, all of which had been concealed by the darkness named ignorance.

These 25 mental properties beginning from faith and ending in reason or insight are known as morally beautiful mental properties, as they exist only in such classes of consciousness. These 52 properties though included in one chapter were classified by Anuruddha Thera under 9 classes. The reason for doing so could easily be understood by the reader without a description in detail when the specific functions each class performed are grasped.

HOW CLASSES OF CONSCIOUSNESS ROOTED IN LUST ARISE

According to the teaching in sub-commentary. "yadāhi natthi kāmēsu ādinavōttyādinā" (යදාහි නත්ථි කාමේසු ආදීනවෝත්‍යාදිනා), when one is under the erroneous impression that no harm arises from gratifying the five senses, or "නත්ථි සුකට දුක්කටානං කම්මානං ඵලං විපාකො" (Natthi sukaṭa dukkatānan kammānan phalan vipākō) under the more heinous erroneous belief in that there are no fruits or results from good or bad actions, and automatically of his own accord, without being determined by a second person or without being impelled by a previous consciousness, accompanied by joy indulges in gratifying the senses from the five sense objects, viz. any visual object, sound, smell, taste and touch, or thinks that success or failure depends on seeing good or bad objects such as confronting milk cows and funerals respectively, or hearing pleasant or unpleasant sounds early morning, or smelling a fragrant flower or perfume, or dressing a new suit of clothes, or eating milk rice with ghee and so on, (none of which comes under the 38 actions in Mangala Sutta), or, as taught in the vēdas, going in a particular kind of conveyance, or without paying attention to the law of cause and effect, erroneously believing that fortune depends on the performance of rites and rituals such as bali ceremonies, offering of food, flowers, incense and so on to the planets and dēvas, then the first class of consciousness called automatic consciousness accompanied by joy and connected with error arises.

THOUGHT PROCESS

When that consciousness arises a thought process consisting of seven apperceptions (ජවන javana) results. In one mental act of sense-perception indicated by the words " I see a flower " four processes have to be distinguished, viz.

(1) vision (chakkhudvāra vīthi චක්ඛුවාර වීථි).

(2) Reproductive sequel (තත්තනුවත්තක මනොවාර වීථි tattanuvattaka manōdvāra vīthi).

(3) Conceiving the name (nāma paññatti vīthi නාමපඤ්ඤත්ති වීථි).

(4) Discerning the meaning of the name (attha paññatti vīthi අත්ථ පඤ්ඤත්ති වීථි).

Of these four processes the first three contain apperceptions which are only kamma (actions) and the fourth which discerns the meaning of the name contain apperceptions which are kamma patha (strong enough to cause rebirth in any plane of existence). The first apperceptional volition in the fourth process, having been accompanied by the first three and related to them by the correlations of contiguity, immediate contiguity, absence and abeyance, called kamma or volitional activity, only produces results during the span of life in this existence. The seventh can produce results in the next existence both as rebirth consciousness and as resultant effect during the span of life. The remaining five apperceptions between the two are capable of giving effect, as opportunity occurs, both rebirth and resultant effects during the span of life or only resultant effects during the span of life, according to circumstances, in the wheel of Sansāra or machine of existence.

In the manner in which the 1st class of immoral consciousness is described, the remaining 10 classes of immoral consciousness with the exception of the one associated with distraction, and the 8 classes of moral consciousness should be adjusted.

HOW CLASSES OF CONSCIOUSNESS ROOTED IN AVERSION OR HATE ARISE

According to sub-commentary " dvinnan pana nēsan cittānan pānātipātādīsu tikkha mandappavatti kālē uppatti vēditabbō " (විතතං පන නෙසං චිතතානං පාණාතිපාතාදිසු තිකඛ මනදපපවතති කාලෙ උපපතති වෙදිතබබො), when an unpleasant object is seen, and the immoral act of killing is done automatically without being determined by a second person or without being impelled by a previous consciousness, or when harsh or abusive words are spoken, or immoral ideas arise such as hatred and doing harm to others, the first class of automatic immoral consciousness accompanied by grief and rooted in aversion or hate arises. Similarly, the second volitional class accompanied by grief and rooted in aversion or hate arises, when it is determined by another person or when stimulated by a preceding state of consciousness.

As the sub-commentary states " yan kinci aniṭṭhālambanan navavidha āghāta vatthūni ca dōmanassassa kāranan patighassa kārananacāti daṭṭhabban " (යංකිඤ්චි අනිට්ඨාලම්බනං නවවිධ ආඝාතවත්ථූනි ච දොමනසසසස කාරණං. පටිඝසස කාරණ චායි දට්ඨබබං) confronting an unpleasant object and the nine types of hate bases, are the causes of origination of the two states of grief and hate. If grief and hate were to arise from one cause, then would it not be sufficient when either grief or hate is shown ? The reason for stating grief is because in the other classes too feeling differentiated them and the same rule was followed here in giving both grief and hate.

This class of consciousness arises in committing the immoral acts of killing, using harsh and abusive language, hate, stealing, speaking falsehood, gossiping, and indulging in idle talk.

If immoral acts like killing, using harsh and abusive language, and hate are caused by hate bases which are unpleasant, when one desires to kill and eat the flesh of a fowl, how does a fowl become an unpleasant object ? Of the nine hate bases, which base is obtained in killing and eating the flesh of a fowl is a question that should be asked. When a thought arises to eat the flesh of a fowl, the enemy that opposes the realisation of that idea is the psychic life of the fowl. Therefore the psychic life becomes an unpleasant object. It is obtained in that hate base called " anatthan mē acari " (අනත්තං මෙ අචරි). Therefore the consciousness that arises in a person who kills animals for the purpose of eating the flesh is one rooted in hate or aversion supplemented by greed (lōbha paccaya dōsa moolika cittan ලොභ පච්චය දොස මූලික චිත්තං).

How do the immoral acts of stealing, speaking falsehood, carrying tales and indulgence in idle and unprofitable talk originate in consciousness rooted in hate or aversion? When a thought arises that by taking what is not given from an enemy he could be harmed then it is one rooted in hate or aversion. Similarly, giving false evidence in Law Courts against an enemy, carrying tales with a view to breaking the friendship which exists with an enemy, indulging in such talk as would be causing either a loss or insult to an enemy arise from the root cause of hate or aversion.

HOW CLASSES OF CONSCIOUSNESS ROOTED IN NESCIENCE ARISE

The commentary Atthasālini states " chasu ārammanēsu vēdanā vasēna majjhattassa kankhā pavatti kālē uppajjati " (ඡසු ආරම්මනෙසු වෙදනාවසෙන මජ්ඣත්තස්ස කඞ්ඛා පවත්ති කාලෙ උප්පජ්ජති). Whenever perplexity or doubt arises accompanied by a neutral sensation in regard to the six objects such as visual object and so on, then that consciousness is known as that which is accompanied by indifference and conjoined with perplexity or doubt.

As the commentary Atthasālini states, " idan cittan chasu ārammanēsu vēdanādi vasēna majjhattan hutvā uddhatan hōti " (ඉදං චිත්තං ඡසු ආරම්මනෙසු වෙදනාදිවසෙන මජ්ඣත්තං හුත්වා උද්ධතං හොති). Whenever distraction or restlessness accompanied by a neutral sensation arises in respect of the six objects such as visual object and so on, that consciousness is known as that which is accompanied by indifference and conjoined with distraction or restlessness.

Of these two classes the first one conjoined with perplexity or doubt has the potency to cause rebirth in the four planes of misery and resultant effects during the span of life, and in the seven planes of fortunate sense experience, only the resultant effects during existence.

The second one conjoined with distraction or restlessness is incapable of giving rebirth in any plane, but, nevertheless, it causes resultant effects in planes of misery or those of fortunate sense-experience.

Of these 12 classes of immoral consciousness, 8 are rooted in lust or greed and nescience, 2 are rooted in hate or aversion and nescience and 2 have only one root namely nescience.

Whenever consciousness rooted in lust or greed arises, the face changes colour becoming red like a very ripe nuga fruit (banyan), when one rooted in hate or aversion arises, the face becomes dark like a ripe jambu fruit. Whenever one rooted in nescience arises the face becomes the colour of sesame oil. Therefore from one's physiognomy, the type of consciousness could be ascertained.

IMMORAL RESULTANT CLASSES

UNACCOMPANIED BY HĒTUS

Out of the 18 classes of consciousness unaccompanied by hētus (හෙතු) 7 classes of immoral resultants are obtained from each of the 12 classes of immoral consciousness by way of result or effect. In the event of any action being done by the first class of immoral consciousness accompanied by joy and connected with error, it would cause rebirth in the four planes of misery and give rise to resultant effects during the span of life, and in planes of fortunate sense-experience, only resultant effects. How does it do so? Of the seven classes of immoral resultants, that investigating class of consciousness accompanied by neutral sensation (upēkkhā sahagata santīrana cittan උපෙක්ඛා සහගත සන්තීරණ චිත්තං), having obtained asynchronous volitions from the correlation of kamma belonging to the immoral consciousness, arises in the four planes of misery by way of rebirth. Thereafter, when hideous looking and unpleasant objects such as figures and fires are seen, eye cognition arises through the eye-door by way of effect, immediately following and contiguous to it by way of receiving the objects immoral resultant called the recipient consciousness, next following and contiguous to it by way of investigating the objects the first investigating consciousness, which appeared as rebirth consciousness, arises now functioning as investigating consciousness.

Similarly, when unpleasant words are heard such as " assault, kill " and other harsh and abusive language, auditory consciousness resulting from immoral deeds arises, and similarly the remaining ones, for instance, immoral resultant of olfactory consciousness arises when abominable and offensive smell which is unbearable comes within the avenue of the organ of sense, and in like manner immoral resultant of gustatory consciousness arises when the unhappy and miserable beings are laid on their backs, mouths opened with huge iron bars, and boiling water and red hot iron balls are placed to be drunk and eaten respectively. Again immoral resultant of tactile cognition accompanied by pain arises when they are placed on red hot iron floors and divided into fours, eights, and sixteens, or placed in red hot iron conveyances and assaulted with thorny sticks and taken to the angāra pabbata (charcoal rock).

BASE OF EYE CONSCIOUSNESS

What is the base that eye consciousness depends on? Of the two, the eye-ball which is formed of the four great essentials in which the element of extension predominates, and the sensitive material quality of the eye which is a material quality derived from the four great essentials, the eye consciousness arises depending on the eye base or the sensitive material quality of the eye. The eye-ball is a physical substance or matter formed from the four great material qualities in the ultimate and highest sense. Together with colour, taste, smell and nutritive essence, the eight are called inseparables. Therefore it will be seen that even what is known as matter in the highest and ultimate sense is constituted of the eight inseparables which are only qualities. The sensitive material quality of the eye is a material quality derived from the four great essentials which originated in this existence in the body as a result of a moral act in kāmalōka in a previous existence such as the offering of a visual object through craving for visual objects. This sensitive material quality exists diffused through the seven membranes like sesame oil filtered through seven layers of cotton, behind the region of the pupil in the cornea surrounded by the sclerotic. When the sensitive material quality of the eye is rolled into a ball it is of the size of the head of a louse. Whenever a visual object appears in front of the sensitive material quality, the eye consciousness originating from this base perceives the sense impression. In this sensitive material quality there is a group (kalāpa කලාප) of ten, formed of the eight inseparables, sensitive material quality of the eye and psychic life, which is known as the 'eye-decad.'

BASE OF AUDITORY CONSCIOUSNESS

What is the base on which auditory consciousness depends? It depends on the sensitive material quality of the ear, which is derived from the four great material qualities that exist in the internal ear as the result of giving owing to craving for sounds by way of charity sounds in a previous existence. Inside the external ear, that is in the internal ear, there exists a very fine and delicate hair resembling a copper coloured ring in which the sensitive material quality of the ear exists in a state of diffusion like oil. The auditory consciousness which arises depending on this base perceives sounds. This base is constituted of the eight inseparables, sensitive material quality of the ear, and vital force which form a group known as the 'ear-decad.'

BASE OF OLFACTORY CONSCIOUSNESS

What is the base on which olfactory consciousness depends? It depends on the sensitive material quality of the nose derived from the four great essentials that exist in the body as a result of the performance of a moral act in a previous existence by way of offering sweet scents owing to craving for smell. Inside the nose a state of oil is present diffused through resembling the shape of a goat's hoof. Olfactory consciousness depending on this base arises whenever a good or bad smell comes within its avenue, and perceives the impression of smell. This base which is formed of the eight inseparables, sensitive material quality of smell and vital force constitute a group known as 'nose-decad.'

BASE OF GUSTATORY CONSCIOUSNESS

What is the base on which gustatory consciousness depends? It depends on the sensitive material quality of the tongue derived from the four great essentials existing in the body as the result of the performance of a moral act in a previous existence, such as giving sapids by way of charity, owing to craving for sapids. In the middle of the tongue there exists diffused through a site resembling the end of a lotus flower the sensitive material quality of the tongue resembling oil. Gustatory consciousness depending on this arises whenever any taste comes in contact with the tongue, and perceives the impression of taste. This base which is formed of the eight inseparables, sensitive material quality of the tongue and vital force constitute the group known as 'tongue-decad.'

BASE OF TACTILE CONSCIOUSNESS

What base does tactile consciousness depend on? It depends on the sensitive material quality of the body, with the exception of the ends of hair, down, nails, epithelial scales of the body, and heat evolving from metabolism both internal and external, derived from the four great essentials of the body which have originated by reason of a moral act performed in the past existence as giving by way of charity a tangible object owing to craving for tangible objects. This sensitive material quality exists diffused through the body as something resembling oil. Whenever an unpleasant tangible object comes in contact with it, then tactile consciousness accompanied by pain arises and perceives the sense impression. This base is formed of the eight inseparables, sensitive material quality of the body and vital force of psychic life and constitutes the group known as 'body-decad.'

ILLUSTRATIONS SHOWING THE ARISING OF FIVE DOOR SENSE-IMPRESSIONS

How could the arising of the five-door sense-impressions be illustrated? Just as a sound arises when a drum is struck with a stick, so do the five sense impressions arise when the five sense fields come in contact with the five sensory organs. That the sensitive material quality is like the face of the drum, contact of the five sense objects is like striking the drum with a stick, and the five sense-impressions like the sound of the drum, should be understood. It can easily be understood if one were to think as to how fire arises on striking a match stick on a box of matches.

These five sensitive material qualities are like five blind strong men possessed of their limbs and other organs, and the five classes of consciousness that are dependent on the five bases are like five deformed and limbless men possessing eye sight. Just as, when the limbless man gets on the back of the blind strong man, both could reach any destination they desire, so could the five classes of consciousness, which depend on the five blind sensitive material qualities, perceive the sense impressions like their reaching the desired destination.

RECIPIENT AND INVESTIGATING CONSCIOUSNESS

In a process of thought the state of consciousness immediately following and contiguous to the five classes of sense cognition is known as the recipient consciousness. It first receives the impressions already perceived by them, and the one following next is investigating consciousness, which has the function of investigating what is received and coming to a decision.

When unpleasant objects such as visual object and so on come within the avenue of the five doors immoral resultant consciousness of eye, ear, nose, tongue, and body arise, and also the immoral resultant recipient consciousness and investigating consciousness.

Whenever any of the immoral classes of consciousness with the exception of that accompanied by distraction gives rise to rebirth in the four planes of misery, this immoral resultant investigating consciousness performs the three functions of rebirth, life continuum and redecease. During the span of life the seven classes of immoral resultants arise, according to circumstances, from all the twelve classes of immoral consciousness by way of resulting effects.

SEVEN IMMORAL RESULTANTS

In the seven planes of fortunate sense experience, these seven immoral resultants arise from immoral acts done in the past in any subsequent existence.

With the exception of the realm of unconscious beings, in the other 15 Brahmalokas immoral resultants of visual consciousness and auditory consciousness, recipient and investigating results arise. These occur when the Brahmas view the world of men or come thereto, and as results of immoral acts done in previous existences.

EIGHT MORAL RESULTANTS

When a pleasant object comes within the avenue of the sense doors then the eight classes of moral resultants such as visual consciousness and so on arise, as a result of moral deeds done in previous existences.

INEFFECTIVE CLASSES

Five door turning to impressions arises when either an unpleasant or a pleasant object comes in contact with any of the five doors such as eye door and so on, by way of directing the attention of consciousness to the sense impressions. This is also known as kriyā manō dhātu (ක්‍රියා මනෝධාතු) or ineffective element of mind.

Mind-door turning to impressions is known as manō viññāna dhātu (මනෝ විඤ්ඤාණ ධාතු) or element of mind cognition. It is the 19 classes of consciousness that arise as the life continuum (bhavanga භවංග), which turn to objects perceived by the five classes of sense impressions as sight, hearing, odour, taste and touch.

Consciousness of aesthetic pleasure is that which makes an Arahat laugh over subtle objects and so on.

HOW THE EIGHT CLASSES OF MORAL CONSCIOUSNESS ARISE

(1) Out of the morally beautiful classes of consciousness, the features of the first great class are thus :—As the sub-commentary states, " yadā pana yō deyyadhamma patiggāhakādi sampattin " (යදා පනයොදෙය්‍ය ධම්ම පටිග්ගාහකාදි සම්පත්ති) and so on, whenever suitable articles for offering and suitable recipients are fortunately present and one were to give charity or observe the eight precepts or perform any other moral act with pleasure and heedful of the resulting effects that will doubtless take place, that is connected with knowledge (kammassakata ñāna කම්මස්සකත ඤාණ), and when undetermined by another person or unstimulated by a preceding state of consciousness, then the first class of moral consciousness known as automatic consciousness accompanied by joy and connected with knowledge arises.

(2) As stated in respect of the first class, when any moral action is done such as giving charity and so on with pleasure and connected with knowledge in the belief that all mental actions have resulting effects and determined by a second person, when the individual delays to perform this act owing to craving for possessions, who is a good friend and who states that a person of your position should not be without giving alms and all the fortune you enjoy in this existence is due to your having given alms in previous existence, or having seen others giving alms, he makes up his mind to do the same, that is, impelled by a preceding state of consciousness, then the second class known as volitional consciousness accompanied by joy and connected with knowledge arises.

(3) Children, who had seen alms being given by their parents, no sooner than they encounter a Bhikkhu, would with pleasure offer anything in their possession, or having been taught by parents they salute a priest with great reverence by keeping the hands raised well above the head with the fingers together and in apposition, the two forearms and the two legs in apposition with the head inclined downwards, then the third class known as automatic consciousness accompanied by joy and disconnected from knowledge arises.

(4) Whenever parents enjoin a child to offer this to the Bhikkhu or salute him with reverence, and such orders are carried out with pleasure, then the fourth class known as volitional consciousness accompanied by joy and disconnected from knowledge arises.

(5) Whenever, by reason of one being not so fortunate as to possess suitable offerings or recipients, he with indifference and connected with knowledge in the belief that giving alms brings in good results, undetermined by a second person or unstimulated by a previous state of consciousness, very often by reason of the practice in previous existences, gives alms or performs any other moral act, then the fifth class known as Automatic consciousness accompanied by indifference and connected with knowledge arises.

(6) Whenever the same act as stated in respect of the 5th class is performed, being determined by a second person or impelled by a previous state of consciousness, then the sixth class known as volitional consciousness accompanied by indifference and connected with knowledge arises.

(7) Whenever, owing to a child being not so fortunate as to own suitable offerings or recipients and having seen his parents performing moral acts, he automatically gives anything he possesses to a Bhikkhu or salutes him with reverence, then the seventh class known as Automatic consciousness accompanied by indifference and disconnected from knowledge arises.

(8) When alms are given as stated in class seven, and not automatically but being enjoined to do so by his parents, then the 8th class called volitional consciousness accompanied by indifference and disconnected from knowledge arises.

In the four automatic and volitional classes of consciousness disconnected from knowledge an illustration of a child was given. Then the question may be asked as to whether such classes of consciousness occur only amongst the children. The answer is in the negative. Similar classes can occur amongst adults, old people and even amongst the learned who possess ordinary knowledge and wisdom, but not right views with regard to the inevitable resulting fruits that accrue from giving alms or doing any other moral act or at a time when the act is done without thinking of the resulting effects.

ILLUSTRATION SHOWING THE ORIGINATION OF FIRST CLASS OF MORAL CONSCIOUSNESS

When an individual thinks of giving alms and begins collecting the articles for offering and searching for the Bhikkhus who are to be the recipients, then an incalculable number of thought processes, each containing seven apperceptions (ජවන javana), takes place during that period. On the day and at the time of placing the offerings on the hands of the recipients, the process of thought which occasions the origination of the medium of communication by body by means of which the offerings are made, is called the path of moral act by way of charity, (dānamayan kusalan kammapathan දානමයං කුසලං කම්මපථං), that is the volitional activity that possesses energy to cause rebirth in the seven planes of fortunate sense experience and to be amply rewarded in the form of wealth during his span of existence. Thereafter, every time he thinks of the moral act done, the amount of good moral actions or thought processes is also incalculable. The processes of thought that originate before and after the performance of the act add greater strength to the kamma done, and now the volitional activity is capable of giving a Ti-hētuka paṭisandhi of the higher type (උක්කට්ඨං ukkaṭṭhan) or rebirth associated with the three roots of disinterestedness, amity and knowledge. Of the seven apperceptions or javana (ජවන), the first has its fruits in this existence itself as resultant effects in the form of immense wealth such as were enjoyed by Dhananjaya, Mendaka and so on during the past, the seventh one causes rebirth in any realm of fortunate sense experience in the following existence and also resultant effects during the span of life there, such as was provided for Ankura dēvaputta and so on. The remaining five volitions present in the apperceptions are capable of effecting both rebirth and resultant effects either in kāmalōka, Rūpa or Arūpalokas, as circumstances permit, for indefinite periods. Even after the extinction of a kappa (aeon) and when opportunity affords, one can even after departing from an existence in the worst plane of misery, be born in any of the six dēvalōkas, develop the fourth stage of jhāna from the kasina circle of air and be born again in the Brahmalōkas.

This first great class of consciousness arises in this world of men in Bodhisattas born for the last time, whose kammic force at rebirth is sufficient to live for an asankheyya (අසංඛෙය්‍ය) incalculable number of years. Although such is the case, as our Gautama Bodhisatta was born during the decadence of a kappa when physical conditions were unsuitable for long life, he was only able to live for the very short period of 80 years.

REASON FOR CALLING THIS CLASS OF MORAL CONSCIOUSNESS "GREAT"

Why is the adjective "great" used before these classes of consciousness when the sublime states of consciousness in Rūpa and Arūpalōka and transcendental consciousness are progressively higher classes? The answer is that the word maha (මහා) "great" is used because these classes have a wider and more extensive field for rebirth and resultant effects, whereas the higher classes are only capable of effecting results in particular realms according to the stages of Jhāna developed, and the paths entered. These eight classes of moral consciousness give rise to rebirth and resulting effects during the span of life in the seven planes of fortunate sense experience and resultant effects in the eleven planes of Kāmalōka existence. Therefore, there is no other class of consciousness, than the great moral classes of consciousness, that has such an extensive and wide field for effects to take place.

HOW THE EIGHT MORAL CLASSES BECOME ENDLESS AND INCALCULABLE

Although the eight great classes of moral consciousness, four of which are accompanied by joy and four by indifference, are described as eight, they become 15,120 when reckoned by way of the five places where they can originate. How is this reckoned?

"Kamēna puññavatthūhi gōcarādhipatīhica.
Kamma heenāditōcēva ganeyya naya kōvidō"

"කමෙන පුඤ්ඤවත්ථූහි ගොචරාධිපතීහිච
කම්ම හීනාදිතොචෙව ගණෙය්‍ය නය කොවිදො"

According to this stanza the calculation should be made. When the eight classes of great moral consciousness are multiplied by the ten kinds of moral acts, viz charity, morality, concentration, transferring of merit to others, receiving merit from others, hearing the doctrine, preaching the doctrine, reverence, service, and steps taken to form correct views, they become eighty. When that number is multiplied by the six fields of sense viz. visual object, sound, smell, sapids, touch and cognizable object, they become 480 classes. Of these, when the 240 classes accompanied with knowledge are multiplied by the four steps to Iddhi potency (viz desire-to-do), mind, effort and investigation they become 960 classes. When the 240 classes disconnected from knowledge are multiplied by three of the steps to Iddhi potency, viz desire-to-do, mind, and effort, they become 720 classes. When these two classes are added they become 1,680. This number when multiplied by the three doors through which all moral acts should be performed—viz by body, speech and thought—they become 5,040. When this is multiplied by the three grades of minor, moderate and highest, they become 15,120 classes.

In the commentary, written by Buddnadatta Ācāriya, called the Abhidhamma Avatāra, the following verse appears—

" Sattarasa sahassāni dvēsatāni asītica
Kāmāvacara puññāni bhavantīti viniddisē

සත්තරස· සහස්සානි වෙසතානි අසීතිච
කාමාවචර පුඤ්ඤානි භවන්තීති විනිද්දිසෙ "

According to this, 17,280 moral states of consciousness are said to occur. This discrepancy is due to the 240 classes of consciousness disconnected from knowledge being reckoned under the four steps to Iddhi potency, when the fourth step of investigation is not present in such classes.

When the 15,120 classes are multiplied by time such as past, present and future, and by different places, the number becomes endless and incalculable.

The eight classes of great ineffective consciousness should be similarly reckoned.

HOW THE EIGHT GREAT MORAL RESULTANTS BECOME ENDLESS AND INCALCULABLE

The sub-commentary states "imānipi iṭṭha iṭṭha majjhattārammana vasēna yathākkaman sōmanassa upēkkhā sahitāni" (ඉමානිපි ඉට්ඨ ඉට්ඨමජ්ඣත්තාරම්මන වසෙන යථාක්කමං සොමනස්ස උපෙක්ඛා සහිතානි). When a moral consciousness arises from a very pleasant object, the resultant consciousness would be accompanied by joy, and when it arises from a moderately pleasant object, then the resultant consciousness would be accompanied with indifference. What are the causes of the resultants being connected with knowledge and disconnected from knowledge? When the kamma force which gives rise to rebirth is intense, then rebirth consciousness which appears as a resultant is accompanied with knowledge, and when the kamma force is feeble and yet gives rise to rebirth, then the resultant rebirth consciousness is disconnected from knowledge.

When the great resultant consciousness appears as retention consciousness (tadālambana තදාලම්බන) it will be very often connected with knowledge or disconnected from knowledge according as the previous javana vīthi (ජවන වීථි) or process of apperception is connected with knowledge or disconnected from knowledge. But this does not take place invariably and as a rule. Why so? Because an individual whose rebirth consciousness is connected with knowledge, and whose life continuum (bhavanga භවංග) is also as such, whenever apperceptions disconnected from knowledge arise, by reason of the force of the previous life continuum (bhavanga භවංග) retention consciousness can be connected with knowledge.

Similarly, an individual whose rebirth consciousness is disconnected from knowledge can have a retention consciousness disconnected from knowledge, even when it follows apperceptions connected with knowledge.

REBIRTH CONSCIOUSNESS

By the force of the eight great moral classes of consciousness, according to circumstances, rebirth can be caused by any one of the nine classes of consciousness capable of giving rebirth in kāmalōka excluding the four planes of misery.

To one who obtains rebirth in any sphere of fortunate sense-experience from an intense and great moral consciousness, eight resultants conditioned by roots and eight resultants unconditioned by roots take place during the span of life. When rebirth occurs from one of the great resultants connected with knowledge, as resultant effects one gets immense wealth in the form of gold, silver, jewels, cattle, horses, landed property and so on.

An individual, who is born with rebirth consciousness conditioned by two roots (duhētuka ද්වෙහෙතුක) and disconnected from knowledge, can obtain wealth of a moderate degree by his own effort such as doing agriculture, trade and so on. One, who is born from a feeble moral consciousness disconnected from knowledge, is born blind or defective in any of the sensory organs or deformed and so on, and as resultant effects one has to work as a servant or engage himself in low type of work such as fishing, hunting and so on. During the span of life he only obtains as resultant effects the eight moral resultants unconditioned by roots. As the latter has no good resultant effects he is compelled to lead a miserable life. In Rūpalōka, excepting unconscious beings, those in the other fifteen planes obtain only the four good resultants of visual consciousness, auditory consciousness, recipient consciousness and investigating consciousness unconditioned by roots.

CHŪLANĀGA CONTROVERSY

According to the controversy by Chūlanāga Thēro, out of the four great moral classes of consciousness conditioned by the three roots and which are of the highest degree, one gives rise to rebirth in the form of a great moral resultant consciousness conditioned by the three roots out of the four classes of resultant consciousness. During the span of life 16 resultants arise, eight being great moral resultants conditioned by their roots and eight unconditioned by their roots. Out of the four great moral classes of consciousness conditioned by the three roots but which are feeble, any one of them resembles in power one out of the four great moral classes conditioned by only two roots but of the highest degree. Therefore, when rebirth occurs from a feeble ti-hētuka or the highest duhētuka, that is, connected with the three roots which are feeble or two roots which are very high, it is a great moral resultant disconnected from knowledge out of the four such resultants that arises as rebirth consciousness. During the span of life twelve resultants are obtained, namely, four great resultants disconnected from knowledge and eight unconditioned by roots. When a feeble great moral consciousness connected with two roots, out of the four such classes, causes rebirth, it is the moral resultant known as investigating consciousness accompanied by indifference that arises as rebirth consciousness. During the span of life only the eight resultants unconditioned by roots are obtained.

Although the great resultants are eight they become innumerable and incalculable when reckoned in the following manner. They become 80 when the ten classes of moral acts are reckoned. These become 480 when the six sensory objects are taken into account. They become 1,440 when the three doors of body speech and thought are reckoned. They become 4,320 when each act is divided into three degrees feeble, moderate and intense. When time and places are reckoned they become endless and incalculable.

Thus the eight great moral classes appear as 15,280, the eight great ineffective classes as 15,280, and the eight great resultants as 4,320 as far as the range of calculation goes.

EIGHT GREAT INEFFECTIVE CLASSES

BELONGING TO THE ARAHANTS

The commentary Atthasālini states "tan tan kiccasādhana vasēna pavattā pana kārana matta mēva hoti tasmā kriyāvuttā" (තං. තං. කිච්චසාධන වසෙන පවත්තා පන කාරණ මත්ත මෙව හොති තස්මා ක්‍රියාවුත්තා). Although such and such an action is done, as it is incapable of producing results, any action done such as giving alms and so on is only a mere action and it is called ineffective. Atthasālini further states "idan cittan aññēsan asādhāranan khīnāsavassēva pāṭi puggalikan chasu dvārēsu labbhati" (ඉදං. චිත්තං. අඤ්ඤෙසං. අසාධාරණං. ඛීණාසවස්සෙව පාටිපුග්ගලිකං. ඡසු ද්වාරෙසු ලබ්භති). This group of ineffective classes of consciousness is not obtained by the worldings and those who have attained the paths and fruitions up to the Never-returners (Anāgamis). They only arise in the Arahants, Paccēka Buddhas and Buddhas, who have totally extinguished all the āsavās (defilements, torments and so on). Similar to the moral classes of consciousness, the ineffective classes originate through the six doors.

The three classes of moral, resultant and ineffective consciousness, may be compared to a mango tree. The great moral consciousness is like a ripe seed fit for germination, and ineffective consciousness is like a ripe seed unfit for germination and therefore not producing a tree, and the great resultant class is like the fruits that appear on the tree.

SYNTHESIS OF MENTAL PROPERTIES OF CONSCIOUSNESS IN RŪPALŌKA AND ARŪPALŌKA

In the 27 classes of sublime consciousness made up of 15 of rūpa and 12 of Arūpa consciousness, all the mental properties obtained in kāmalōka consciousness with the exception of the three Abstinences arise in the three classes of 1st stage of Jhāna. Therefore, 35 mental properties arise in 1st stage of Jhāna. In the three classes of 2nd stage of Jhāna with the exception of initial application there are 34. In the three classes of 3rd stage of Jhāna there are 33, excluding both initial and sustained application. In the 3 classes of the 4th stage of Jhāna 32 are obtained excluding initial application, sustained application and pleasurable interest. In the 15 classes of the 5th stage of Jhāna, eliminating initial application, sustained application, pleasurable interest, pity and appreciation, 30 mental properties are obtained. When one wishes to ascertain what mental properties are associated with and what not associated with classes of sublime consciousness, the three abstinences must always be totally eliminated. The reason for this being that the abstinences come under purity of morals, which has to be completed before purity of mind in the form of Jhāna takes place. The five mental properties not arising in the 5th stage of Jhāna, arise in some and not in other Jhānas. Therefore one must ascertain the differences existing between the different classes of consciousness by taking initial application, sustained application, pleasurable interest, pity and appreciation into consideration.

SYNTHESIS OF MENTAL PROPERTIES IN RŪPALŌKA CONSCIOUSNESS

Vibhangappakarana states "Jhānanti vitakkō vicārō pīti sukhan cittēkaggatā" (ඣානන්ති විතක්කො විචාරො පීති සුඛං චිත්තෙකග්ගතා). Initial application, sustained application pleasurable interest, pleasure and one-pointedness are the five factors of Jhāna. Each of these, individually taken, is called a factor of Jhāna, but not Jhāna itself. When all the five factors arise in one state of consciousness, then it is called Jhāna. If such be the case, how is it that when four, three or two factors are associated with consciousness, they too become Jhānas? When the two factors of equanimity and one-pointedness are associated with consciousness, they themselves perform the functions of the other three factors. Therefore, consciousness which is associated with two factors also is Jhāna. How do the five properties of initial application and so on become Jhāna factors? sacca sankhēpa states:—

"Upanijjhāna kiccattā kāmādi paṭipakkhitō
Santēsupica aññēsu pancēvajhāna saññitā"

"උපනිජ්ඣාන කිච්චත්තා කාමාදි පටිපක්ඛිතො
සන්තෙසුපිච අඤ්ඤෙසු පඤ්චෙවඣාන සඤ්ඤිතා"

Because these five factors of initial application and so on are associated with the 1st Jhāna consciousness, which consists in all of 35 mental properties, it is called a Jhāna. Then, if only these five are Jhāna factors, is one justified in calling the other 30 mental properties and consciousness as belonging to Kāmalōka? Or is there another designation for them in Rūpalōka? Just as many ingredients used for a curry after boiling become a curry by the force of heat, even so the other 30 mental properties associated with consciousness containing the five Jhāna factors become Jhāna by the force of the five Jhāna factors. Initial application and so on are called the Jhāna factors because they view the object from very close quarters and also because they are the opposites of the five hindrances, which are inhibited. The word Jhāna is derived from the root "Jhecintāyan" (ඣෙචින්තායං) "viewing at close quarters." What does it look at at close quarters? It looks at the transformed after-image (paṭibhāga nimitta

පටිභාග නිමිත්ත) of kasina circles and so on at close quarters. How does it look at the object at close quarters? When 31 blind men and 5 possessing good eyesight are asked to look at a blaze of fire on the top of a mountain in a dark night, those five men who are not blind will see the blaze of fire as it was quite close to them. As it is a dark night, the trees and creepers and so on that are between them and the place of the fire will not be seen. Similarly, the five factors of Jhāna associated with consciousness will, without seeing any other object, only see the transformed after-image (paṭibhāga nimitta). Just as the 31 men who are blind are unable to see the blaze of fire on the mountain, so are the 30 mental properties such as contact and so on and the Jhāna consciousness with which they are associated unable to see the bright and fiery appearance of the transformed after-image (paṭibāgha nimitta පටිභාග නිමිත්ත).

FUNCTIONS OF JHĀNA FACTORS

The mental property of initial application makes the Jhāna consciousness associated with its adjuncts apply itself initially to the transformed after-image of the kasina circle. Sustained application causes the Jhāna consciousness with its associated adjuncts apply itself in a sustained manner without a break. Pleasurable interest makes the Jhāṇa consciousness and the associated adjuncts pleased at the transformed after-image. Pleasure causes the Jhāna consciousness and the adjuncts which are associated with it happiness over the transformed after-image. The mental property of one-pointedness, having obtained help from the other four factors, keeps itself and the Jhāna consciousness with its adjuncts well established on the transformed after-image and can do whatever it desires with the object. Therefore, the five factors are equally well established on the transformed after-image, without any one of the factors being less or more than the others.

These five factors of the Jhāna become enemies of the five Hindrances that are hostile to them. Initial application, called the lion, is inimical to sloth and torpor, called the elephant. Sustained application called garunda (a kind of hawk) is inimical to perplexity or doubt, called the snake. Pleasurable interest, called the cat, is inimical to ill-will, called the rat. Pleasure, called the snake, is inimical to distraction and worry, called the frog. One-pointedness, called the tiger, is inimical to the sense desires, called the deer. Thus it will be seen that these five factors are able to inhibit the five Hindrances.

HOW JHĀNA CONSCIOUSNESS GIVES RISE TO RESULTS

How does Jhāna consciousness in Rūpalōka produce results? When one who practises mental culture on calm and develops the 1st stage of Jhāna and dies in that state, he would be born in the realm of Brahma's retinue by the resultant consciousness corresponding to the 1st stage of Jhāna. After the expiration of one third of kappa (aeon), he dies and if not reborn in another realm of Brahmalōka, would take rebirth in kāmalōka either with resultant consciousness accompanied by three or two roots according to the moral class of consciousness from which he developed the 1st Jhāna in a previous existence.

RESULTS OF FIRST JHĀNA

When the 1st stage of Rūpalōka Jhāna has been developed and reviewed with two or three of the five reviewing habits and practised, and he dies after practising two or three reviewing habits, he would be born in the realm of Brahma's Ministers and live for half a kappa (aeon), after which if not reborn in another realm of Brahmalōka, would take rebirth in kāmalōka either with resultant consciousness accompanied by three or two roots according to the moral class of consciousness from which he developed the 1st Jhāna in a previous existence.

When the 1st stage of Rūpalōka Jhāna has been developed and well practised in respect of the five reviewing habits, after death he would be born in the realm of Mahā Brahmā and live for one kappa (aeon). After death, if not reborn in another realm of Brahmalōka, he would take rebirth in one of the seven planes of fortunate sense-experience.

According to the commentary Atthasālini "itthiyō pana ariyā vā anariyā vā aṭṭha samāpatti lābhiniyō brahmapāri-sajjēsuyēva nibbattanti" (ඉත්ථියො පන අරියාවා අනාරියාවා අට්ඨ සමාපත්ති ලාභිනියො බ්‍රහ්මපාරි සජ්ජෙසුයෙව නිබ්බ

තාතාති) when women who have attained the first three paths and fruition but not developed any Jhānas and remain as householders and develop the 1st stage of Jhāna just before death, they are reborn in the realm of Brahma's retinue. And so would the women who have developed Jhānas but not attained the paths and fruits. Thereafter, they would progressively develop Jhānas up to the 5th stage and would be reborn time after time in the other realms of Brahmalōka and at last in the realm of Supreme Beings (Akaniṭṭha අකනිට්ඨ) whence they would attain Nibbāna.

RESULTS OF SECOND AND THIRD JHĀNAS

When the 2nd and 3rd stages of Jhāna are developed, rebirth takes place in the realms of minor lustre, of infinite lustre and of the radiant Brahmā, according to the degree of the Jhāna from the view point of the five reviewing habits. Although both the stages effect rebirth in one plane, there would be the difference in their lustre and fortune. If they are incapable after death of being reborn in other realms of Rūpalokā, they would take rebirth in any of the seven planes of fortunate sense experience either with resultant consciousness accompanied with three or two roots according to the nature of moral consciousness in the thought process from which the Jhāna was developed.

RESULTS OF FOURTH JHĀNA

When the 4th stage of Jhāna is developed in a mild, moderate and intense degree, according to the five reviewing habits, rebirth takes place respectively in the realms of the Brahmā of minor aura, of infinite aura and of the Brahmā full of steady aura. After death, if not reborn in any of the other Rūpalōkas, rebirth would be effected in any of the seven planes of fortunate sense experience in the same manner as stated previously.

RESULTS OF FIFTH JHĀNA

When the 5th stage of Jhāna has been developed in a mild, moderate and intense degree, in respect of the five reviewing habits, rebirth takes place in the realm of the Brahmā of great reward. Although their life term is the same, namely, 500

Maha Kappas (aeons), there is a difference in their brilliance according to the degree of cultivating the Jhāna.

The 5th stage of Jhāna could be developed by other than Buddhists who have a ti-hētuka paṭisandhi, that is, rebirth consciousness accompanied by three roots of disinterestedness, amity and knowledge. When those with erroneous ideas and views, seeing the faults of mind and mental concomitants only, desire to inhibit them as "saññā rōgō saññā gandō" (සඤ්ඤා රෝගෝ සඤ්ඤා ගණ්ඩෝ), that is, perception is a disease perception is an abscess, they develop the 5th Jhāna from the kasina circle of air and after death are born in the sphere of unconscious beings in the same attitude as they were on the supervention of the Jhāna with a physical body and appear as a statue. After the expiration of the life term of 500 Maha Kappas, rebirth takes place in Kāmalōka according to kamma done in the existence in which the Jhāna was developed. It should be noted that in this case rebirth does not take place from the moral consciousness occurring in the thought process from which the Jhāna was developed.

The Never-returners after death are born in the five Pure Abodes or in any other realms of Rūpalōka as desired by each. When the controlling power of faculty of faith is very great at the time of developing the fifth Jhāna, rebirth takes place in the abode of the immobile (Aviha අවිහ). When that of mindfulness is very great, rebirth occurs in the abode of the Serene (Atappa අතප්ප). When that of effort is very great, rebirth occurs in the abode of Beautiful (Sudassa සුදස්ස). When that of concentration is very great, rebirth arises in the abode of "clear-sighted" (Sudassī සුදස්සී) and when the controlling power or faculty of reason is very great, rebirth occurs in the abode of Supreme Beings (Akaniṭṭha අකණිට්ඨා).

When Āriyas or those who have attained the paths and fruits are born in the realms of great reward, in the abode of Supreme Beings and in the sphere of neither perception nor no perception, as they are the highest in each class, they will not after death be born in other spheres, but will attain the remaining Paths and fruits and obtain Nibbāna.

"Vēhapphalē akaniṭṭhē bhavaggēca patiṭṭhitā
Na punaññattha jāyanti sabbē ariya puggalā
Brahmalōkagatā heṭṭhā ariyā nōpapajjarē"

"වෙහප්ඵලෙ අකනිට්ඨෙ භවග්ගෙච පතිට්ඨිතා
න පුනඤ්ඤත්ථ ජායන්ති සබ්බෙ අරිය පුග්ගලා
බ්‍රහ්මලොකගතා හෙට්ඨා අරියා නොපපජ්ජරෙ."

So states Anuruddha Ācariya in the analysis of Mind and Body.

HOW RŪPALŌKA CONSCIOUSNESS IS RECKONED

Although the number of classes of moral consciousness in Rūpalōka is stated to be five, the number becomes twenty-five "nines" when reckoned in the following manner. These classes are described as four stages of Jhāna, blending the first Jhāna with the second in respect of highly intelligent people, and as five in respect of the less intelligent class of people. What are the causes of these two ways? As the Jhāna factors associated with the fourth and fifth Jhānas of Rūpalōka and the four classes of Arūpalōka Jhāna resemble each other in respect of the number of Jhāna factors or because these six Jhānas are each associated with two Jhāna factors, these six are classed under the fourth Jhāna/and described as four Jhānas. Although the Jhāna factors associated with these six are alike in number, that in which the two factors of pleasure and one-pointedness are associated is known as the fourth Jhāna and both the fifth Jhāna of Rūpalōka and the four Jhānas of Arūpalōka, which are associated with the two factors of equanimity and one-pointedness in consideration of their Jhāna factors being the same, these five are classed under the fifth Jhāna and described as such.

What is the reason for so describing? They are so described according to the degree of intelligence of the fortunate ones in an audience who are fit to realise the four Āriyan truths. They are described as four to highly intelligent ones and as five to less intelligent ones, as the former could attain their object when facts are stated in a concise manner, but the latter need a detailed description owing to their intelligence being of a lower grade.

When both the four Jhānas and five Jhānas are taken together, they are known as the "pure nine" (suddhika navaka සුද්ධික නවක). As these nine are described including the four types of practices viz (1) unhappy practice with delayed realisation (dukkhā paṭipadā dandhābhiññā දුක්ඛා පටිපදා දන්ධාභිඤ්ඤා) (2) unhappy practice with undelayed realisation (dukkhā paṭipadā khippābhiññā දුක්ඛා පටිපදා ඛිප්පාභිඤ්ඤා) (3) happy practice with delayed realisation (sukhā paṭipadā dandhābhiññā සුඛා පටිපදා දන්ධාභිඤ්ඤා) and happy practice with undelayed realisation (sukhā paṭipadā khippābhiñña සුඛා පටිපදා ඛිප්පාභිඤ්ඤා), each of the four practices will have nine Jhānas. In the moral consciousness belonging to the first Jhāna obtained by unhappy practice and delayed realisation and so on, when the four kinds of practices are included, each of the practices becomes nine classes of Jhānas. These nine are also described under four classes of objects viz (1) minor object in kāmalōka (paritta parittārammana පරිත්ත පරිත්තාරම්මන) (2) unlimited object in kāmalōka (paritta appamānārammana පරිත්ත අප්පමාණාරම්මන) (3) minor object in sublime classes (appamāna parittārammana අප්පමාණ පරිත්තාරම්මන) and (4) unlimited objects in sublime classes (appamāna appamānārammana අප්පමාණ අප්පමාණාරම්මණ) each class of object will have nine Jhānas, as each of the four classes are included in the description of these pure nine.

Thereafter, taking together the four types of objects and the four types of practices the pure nine are described, such as unhappy practice with delayed realisation from a minor object in kāmalōka and so on (dukkhā paṭipadā dandhābhiññā paritta parittārammana දුක්ඛා පටිපදා දන්ධාභිඤ්ඤා පරිත්ත පරිත්තාරම්මණ). Therefore, taking together the object and practice there would be eight of the 'pure nines'. When these eight, the pure nine previously stated, the nines of four practices, and the nines of four objects are taken together there are in all twenty-five nines in a moral consciousness of Rūpalōka. "Dukkhā paṭipadā dandhābhiññan appamānan appamānārammanan" දුක්ඛා පටිපදා දන්ධාභිඤ්ඤං අප්පමාණං අප්පමාණාරම්මණං, that is, unhappy practice with delayed realisation from an unlimited object in sublime classes and so on, the eight types of emancipation, the four Brahma-vihāras, the ten impurities, and so on, when used as subjects for meditation and concentration could produce Rūpalōka Jhānas and their differences could be understood according to the nature of the subjects, for instance, from the ten impurities only the 1st Jhāna could be developed and the first three of the Brahma vihāras only up to the fourth Jhāna and so on.

Resultant and ineffective classes in Rūpalōka, when reckoned in the above manner, are similar to those of moral classes of Jhānas.

MORAL, RESULTANT AND INEFFECTIVE CONSCIOUSNESS OF ARŪPALŌKA

Of the twelve classes of consciousness in Arūpalōka, the moral, resultant and ineffective classes of consciousness, dwelling on the infinity of space, are obtained from space abstracted from the transformed after-image, which has been developed from any of the nine kasina circles excepting space, as space cannot be abstracted from space. This moral consciousness is associated with thirty mental concomitants and equanimity and one-pointedness are the Jhāna factors, as this belongs to the fifth stage of Jhāna. This Arūpa Jhāna dwelling on the infinity of space can be developed by anyone who has not attained the Paths and Fruits as well as by those who have attained the first three Paths and Fruits. After death, resultant consciousness of this Jhāna gives rise to rebirth in the sphere of infinity of space where the life term is 20,000 kappas. The same Jhāna when developed by the Arahants, Paccēka Buddhas and Sammā Sambuddhas, are called ineffective Jhānas.

In the same manner, in respect of the other three Arūpa Jhānas, there are 30 mental concomitants associated with the 2nd Jhāna dwelling on the infinity of consciousness, and so with the 3rd Jhāna dwelling on nothingness, and 4th Jhāna dwelling on neither perception nor no perception. Resultant Consciousness of the 2nd Jhāna gives rise to rebirth in the sphere of infinity of consciousness where the life term is 40,000 kappas, 3rd Jhāna in the sphere of nothingness where the life term is 60,000 kappas and 4th Jhāna in the sphere of neither perception nor no perception where the life term is 80,000 kappas. Each of these could be developed by the four kinds of people referred to above. They are called ineffective when these Jhānas are developed by the Arahants, Paccēka Buddhas and Sammā Sambuddhas.

SYNTHESIS OF MENTAL CONCOMITANTS IN TRANSCENDENTAL CONSCIOUSNESS

In transcendental consciousness there are 36 mental concomitants associated with the 1st stage of Jhāna, 35 with the 2nd stage, 34 with the 3rd stage, and 33 each in 4th and 5th stages.

When transcendental and sublime classes of consciousness are taken together, in the 11 classes of 1st stage of Jhāna there are 38 mental concomitants, in the 11 classes of 2nd stage of Jhāna there are 37, in the 11 classes of 3rd stage of Jhāna 36, in the 11 classes of 4th stage of Jhāna 35, and in the 23 classes of 5th stage of Jhāna 33.

In transcendental consciousness belonging to the path of stream-attainment, the four immoral classes of consciousness connected with error, and that connected with perplexity or doubt will never arise, as the three fetters of error, rite and ritualism and perplexity have been completely extinguished by attaining the stream. The remaining seven classes of immoral consciousness have not the energy to cause rebirth in any of the planes of misery.

In those who have attained the path of once returning, the four classes of immoral consciousness disconnected from error and the two rooted in aversion or hate have not the energy to give rebirth in kāmalōka as beggars and others of low status.

By the path of never-returning the two immoral classes of consciousness rooted in aversion or hate are completely destroyed, and the two fetters of sense desires and ill-will also are destroyed. The four classes of immoral consciousness rooted in greed and disconnected from error are so attentuated as to prevent any attachment to sense desires.

By the Path of Arahatship the four classes of immoral consciousness disconnected from error and that class conjoined with distraction are completely eradicated, together with the remaining five fetters viz desire for Rūpalōka, desire for Arūpalōka, conceit, restlessness and ignorance. Immediately following the paths are the fruits. Two states of consciousness regarding the fruits take place in those of very high intelligence and three with the less intelligent ones. In all the three worlds there is no greater happiness enjoyed than the fruits derived from the paths, for with this human body the bliss of Nibbāna could be realised.

There are no ineffective classes of consciousness connected with transcendental states. The path lasts for one thought moment only and at that time the fetters and torments that should be annihilated by the particular path are done. It is like a tree that has been completely destroyed by lightning. It does not need to be struck again with lightning to prevent the growth. Similarly, as some of the classes of immoral consciousness and the torments are completely exterminated by the different paths, they never arise again. Just as a man in possession of any article that gives him pleasure and happiness could enjoy that sensation every time he looks at it, even so could the Āriya who has attained the Paths and Fruits get into ecstasy whenever he desires (phala samāpatti ඵල සමාපත්ති). The series of states of consciousness in ecstasy are not ineffective classes.

Although the number of Path-consciousness is four according to the Path which it is associated with, when reckoned under the three channels of emancipation, such as empty-release (suññata සුඤ්ඤත), signless release (animitta අනිමිත්ත) and not-hankered-after-release (appanihita අප්පණිහිත) and practices and so on they become innumerable.

HOW TRANSCENDENTAL CONSCIOUSNESS BECOMES INNUMERABLE

The path consciousness in stream attainment becomes eight in number, when it is reckoned as two by way of empty-release and not-hankered-after-release and multiplied by the four kinds of practices viz.

(1) Unhappy practice with delayed realisation (2) unhappy practice with undelayed realisation (3) happy practice with delayed realisation and (4) happy practice with undelayed realisation. These eight together with the two classes of empty-release and not hankered-after-release make in all ten classes of Path-consciousness in stream-attainment. These 10 become 190 when multiplied by 19 adjuncts present in them. They are (1) contemplation of body (2) right effort (3) steps to Iddhi Potency (4) controlling power or faculty (5) force (6) factors pertaining to enlightenment (7) truth (8) calm (9) insight (10) supra-mundane state (11) aggregate (12) senses (13) element (14) food (15) contact (16) feeling (17) perception (18) volition and (19) consciousness or mind. When to these 190 previously stated 10 classes of path consciousness are added, they become 200. These 200 become 800 when reckoned by way of the four steps to Iddhi Potency viz (1) desire to do (2) mind (3) consciousness and (4) investigation. When to these 800 the previously stated 200 which are not controlled by the dominating influences are added, they become 1000. These 1000 classes of path consciousness are obtained by 1000 Āriyas, and no single person can obtain any two of these. The stream winner is said to attain the path in 1000 ways, according to the above manner of calculation.

The paths leading to once-returning, never-returning and Arahatship, similarly obtain 1000 ways each. Therefore, there are 4000 ways taking the four paths together.

These 4000 become 20,000 when reckoned by the five ways of purification viz (1) elimination of some of the Torments not associated with craving by the eight factors of the Noble Path (2) departure from the three root causes of immoral consciousness (3) departure from the immoral classes of consciousness (4) departure from the four Āsavās such as sense desires and so on (5) departure from the mental concomitants associated with the four Āsavās.

Again, when these 4000 classes of path consciousness are multiplied by the five factors of Jhāna present in the first stage of Rūpalōka Jhāna, they become again 20,000.

Further, these 4000 classes of Path-consciousness, when reckoned in consideration of the factors of Jhāna being always present when developed, become another 20,000. Of these three ways of reckoning, the second way, in which only the factors of Jhāna are present, applies to the sukkha vipassaka (සුක්ඛ විපස්සක), one attaining the path without developing the Jhānas. The third way is applied to those who practised exercises in calm and developed the Jhānas (Samathayānika සමථයානික). Therefore, in all 60,000 classes of consciousness are obtained in the four Paths, according to Sacca Vibhanga. Just as a person standing in front of a mirror sees the various constituents of his body in the image, so would the four Fruits of the four Paths have 60,000 classes of consciousness. Therefore, 120,000 classes are obtained in the four paths and four Fruits. When the 120,000 are reckoned according to time and places the number becomes innumerable and incalculable.

HOW TRANSCENDENTAL CONSCIOUSNESS BECOMES FORTY CLASSES

Again, the four Paths and the four Fruits become 20 Paths and 20 Fruits, when reckoned according to the five factors of Jhāna. This is how the 89 classes of consciousness become 121. How does this occur? Of the three methods of developing Jhāna, as transcendental consciousness resembles any one of them, in respect of the five factors of Jhāna, the eight classes of transcendental consciousness become forty.

ATTAINMENT OF PATH FROM JHĀNA

The sub-commentary states as follows:—

" paṭhamajjhānādīsu yan yan jhānan samāpajjitva tatō tatō vuṭṭhāya sankhārē sammasantassa vuṭṭhāna gāmini vipassanā pavattā tan pādakajjhānan nāma "

" පඨමජ්ඣානාදීසු යං යං ඣානං සමාපජ්ජිත්වා තතො තතො වුට්ඨාය සංඛාරෙ සම්මසන්තස්ස වුට්ඨාන ගාමිනී විපස්සනා පවත්තා තං පාදකජ්ඣානං නාම "

When an individual, practising mental culture and concentration, develops any one of the five Jhānas, he maintains it for any length of time he desires and on awaking from same contemplates all conditioned phenomena as impermanent, sorrowful, and lacking a personal entity. When he has come to full maturity of insight, reflection by way of the mind-door suspends the life-continuum and two or three states of consciousness revealing insight concerning any one of the three salient marks occur by name of 'preparation', 'approximation' and 'qualification.' That "knowledge of things as something concerning which to feel indifference" which, when its climax is reached, is coupled with the "knowledge by which one qualifies oneself for the Path" is also described as "Insight that leads to emergence."

After this, the consciousness of the initiate leaning upon Nibbāna occurs, over mastering kinship with the worldly and evolving kinship with the Āriyas.

Immediately after that consciousness the path, namely, consciousness discerning the fact of ill, expelling the fact of its cause, realising the fact of its cessation, cultivating the fact of the way to cessation, descends into the avenue of ecstatic thought. After that Path-Consciousness, two or three states of consciousness of fruition take their course, two in case of less intelligent and three in highly intelligent people. This is the method of attaining the Path from Jhāna. The states of consciousness described above as 'preparation,' 'approximination' and 'qualification' just prior to 'insight leading to emergence constitute the Jhāna factors and the Path is attained therefrom. The Path and Fruits bear the same factors of Jhāna as those from which they are attained.

Out of the three salient marks, only one is realised by the Āriyas obtaining the Paths and Fruits, whereas the Buddhas realise all the three at one and the same time and progressively reach, from the path of stream-attainment, the path of Arahatship and fruits of same. All the different types of wisdom such as omniscience, enlightenment and so on, are ingrained in the Path-consciousness of Arahatship.

EMANCIPATION

When the Path leading to Arahatship is attained, the mental property of insight contemplating soul-lessness and letting go the firm belief in a soul is a channel of emancipation, called the contemplation of emptiness. Insight associated with the Path, Fruits and Nibbāna also bear the same name of 'emptiness.'

Another Āriya contemplating the three salient marks realises the mark of 'signless.' In this case the mental property of insight contemplating impermanence and letting go the sign of hallucination is a channel of emancipation called the 'contemplation' of the signless.' Insight associated with the Path, Fruits and Nibbāna bear the same name of 'signless'.

Another Āriya contemplating the three salient marks realises the mark of the "Not-hankered-after." In this case the mental property of insight contemplating ill or sorrow and letting go that 'hankering-after' which is craving is a channel of emancipation called the 'contemplation of the Not-hankered-after.' Insight associated with the Path, Fruits and Nibbāna bear the same name of 'Not-hankered-after.'

The Path receives three names according to the course taken by 'Insight leading to emergence,' namely, when that insight discerns all conditioned phenomena as without soul, the Path is called "empty release;" when it discerns all conditioned phenomena as impermanent, the Path is called "signless release;" when it discerns all conditioned phenomena as evil, the Path is called "Not-hankered-after release." The Fruit likewise receives these three names according to the three ways of coming into the Path along the avenues of the Path.

Just as the mental property of insight associated with the moment of consciousness known as the 'qualification' in the thought process of the Path receives the names of 'Insight leading to emergence,' 'knowledge of things as something concerning which to feel indifference,' 'Knowledge by which one qualifies oneself for the Path, 'Knowledge by which one qualifies for realising the truths,' so do the three channels of emancipation called the 'contemplation of emptiness,' 'contemplation of the signless' and the 'contemplation of the not-hankered-after,' give the Paths, Fruits and Nibbāna the names of 'empty release' 'signless release' and 'Not-hankered-after release.'

ATTAINMENT OF PATH FROM CONTEMPLATION OF JHĀNA FACTORS

The sub-commentary states "yan yan jhānan sammasantassa sā pavattā tan sammasitajjhānan." (යං යං ඣානං සම්මසනතසස සා පවතතා තං සම්මසිතජඣානං) that is, when an individual, who has developed any of the five Jhānas, without maintaining it contemplates the factors of the Jhāna as impermanent, sorrowful and soul-less, and insight leading to emergence" arises, he is called an Āriya who has attained the paths and Fruits from contemplation of the Jhāna factors, because the necessary insight for attaining the Paths and Fruits was attained by contemplation of the Jhāna factors.

ATTAINMENT OF PATH ACCORDING TO ONE'S DESIRES

The sub-commentary states "Aho! vata me paṭhamajjhāna sadisō maggō pancangikō dutiyajjhānadīsuvā aññatarasadisō caturangikādi bhēdō maggō bhaveyyāti" Ēvaṃ yōgāvacarassa uppannajjhāsayō puggalajjhāsayō nāma" ("අහො! වත මෙ පඨමජඣාන සදිසො මගෙගා පඤචඞගිකො දුතියජඣානා දිසුවා අඤඤතර සදිසො චතුරඞගිකාදි භෙදො මගෙගා භවෙයාාති" එවං යොගාවචරසස උපපනනජඣාසයො පුගගලජඣාසයො නාම"). When any meditator who has cultivated the four Rūpalōka and the four Arūpalōka Jhānas contemplates any particular state as impermanent and so on, and hopes "Oh! it would be excellent if I could attain the Path with the five factors resembling that of first Jhāna, or with those of the 2nd, 3rd, 4th or 5th Jhāna," and as desired by the meditator attains the Path with factors resembling those of any of the Jhānas he hoped for, then he is called one who has attained the Path according to his desires.

When an individual who has cultivated the Jhānas, maintains any one he desires and after awaking contemplates all conditioned phenomena in the Triple-planed universe under the Three

Salient Marks of impermanence and so on and obtains any of the Paths as stream-attainment and so on, then that Path would be associated with such factors as were present in the Jhāna from which he attained the Path.

When an individual attains the Path without maintaining any of the Jhānas but by contemplating as impermanent and so on any of the Jhānas, then that Path would be associated with factors resembling those of the Jhānas which he contemplated as impermanent and so on.

When a meditator, who has cultivated Jhānas, maintains any of them as he desires, and after awaking contemplates as impermanent and so on any of the other Jhānas he desires, and attains any of the Paths, then that Path would be associated with factors resembling either, as desired by the individual, those of the Jhāna from which he attained the Path or from those of the Jhānas he contemplated as impermanent and so on. When one who has no such desires maintains each of the lower Jhānas and after awaking from each contemplates each of the higher Jhānas as impermanent and so on, then the Path that he obtains would be associated with factors resembling those of the Jhānas he contemplated as impermanent and so on.

When one maintains each of the higher Jhānas and after awaking from each contemplates each of the lower ones as impermanent and so on, then that Path he obtains would be associated with factors resembling those of the Jhānas from which he attained the Path.

Whether one has cultivated the Jhānas or not, when he desires to attain the Paths and Fruits, he contemplates all conditioned phenomena in the Triple-planed universe as impermanent and so on, and thereby attains the Paths and Fruits, then they would be associated with factors resembling those of the first Jhāna.

Again, one may attain the Path of stream attainment by way of the Jhānas, the Path of once-returning by way of the contemplation of the factors of Jhāna and the Path of Never-returning by way of the manner in which he desires to attain the Path, and the Path of Arahatship by not attaining any Jhāna and merely by contemplation of one of the three marks as impermanent and so on.

Again, an Āriya can attain one Path by way of one channel of emancipation called " Emptiness, " another Path by another channel called " Signless " and another by the other channel called " Not-hankered-after."

Again, the Ariyas who have attained the Paths and Fruits, when they develop full fruition, (ඵල සමාපත්ති phala samāpatti) could obtain all the three channels of emancipation. An Āriya can one day enjoy full fruition by way of the channel of emancipation called " Emptiness, " on the second day by way of the channel of emancipation called the " Signless " and on the third day by way of the channel of emancipation called the " Not-hankered-after." Or, if one desires to enjoy full fruition three times during a day, he could do so through the three channels of emancipation.

PART III

CHAPTER XIII

Compendium of Particular Concomitants of Consciousness

INTRODUCTORY

" Sampayuttā yathāyogan tepaññāsa sabhāvatō
citta cētasikā dhammā tēsandāni yathārahan[1]
Vēdanā hētutōkiccā dvārālambana vatthutō
Cittuppāda vasēnēva sangahō nāma nīyatē "

"සම්පයුත්තා යථායෝගං තෙපඤ්ඤාස සභාවතො
චිත්ත චෙතසිකා ධම්මා තෙසන්දානි යථාරහං[1]
වෙදනා හෙතුතොකිච්චා ද්වාරාලම්බන වත්ථුතො
චිත්තුප්පාද වසෙනෙව සඞ්ගහො නාම නීයතෙ"

In consciousness and its concomitants there are fifty-three states of consciousness according to the manner in which they are combined. Now, a summary of these will be made by way of thoughts as they arise[1] treating of feeling, of the six hētus, of function, of springing from doors, and having objects and material base.

NOTE I

Yathārahan (යථාරහං), literally, 'according to circumstances,' means that the learner should study, summarize and commit to memory (1) hētus with reference to ahētuka (අහෙතුක) consciousness (2) 'doors' with reference to those classes of consciousness arising through them (3) 'bases' with reference to those classes other than Arūpalōka thoughts which are without 'bases' (4) feeling, function, and objects with reference to all classes.

FEELING

Summarising feeling, in the first place, feeling is three-fold—it is pleasant, painful and neither pleasant nor painful (neutral sensation). Or, again, it may be divided into five[1]— pleasure pain, joy, grief and hedonic indifference.

Note 1

Spoken of as the indriya divisions. Indriya means controlling power or faculty.

Here, among sense impressions, which are the result of moral deeds done in a former birth, there is only one kind that is accompanied by pleasurable feeling and that is tactile impressions[2]. Likewise, there is only one kind of those sense-impressions due to immoral deeds done in a former birth, that is accompanied by painful feeling, and that again is tactile impressions.

Now there are sixty-two kinds of consciousness which are accompanied by joy, to wit :—

(*a*) The eighteen classes of Kāmalōka consciousness which are accompanied by joy—*i. e.* four of the eight appetitives, twelve of the Kāmalōka morally beautiful kinds of consciousness and the two—pleasurable investigation and aesthetic pleasure.

(*b*) The forty-four kinds of sublime and transcendental consciousness termed first, second, third and fourth Jhāna, as each Jhāna obtains 11 classes of consciousness.

But the thoughts accompanied by grief are the only two classes of consciousness connected with aversion or hate.

All the remaining fifty-five classes of consciousness are accompanied by hedonic indifference. They are as follows :—

(*a*) 6 classes of immoral consciousness accompanied by hedonic indifference.

(*b*) 14 classes unaccompanied by hētus and accompanied by hedonic indifference.

(*c*) 12 classes of morally beautiful consciousness in Kāmalōka accompanied by hedonic indifference.

(*d*) 23 classes of sublime and transcendental consciousness belonging to the fifth Jhāna.

NOTE 2

By tactile impressions, Kāyika sukha (කායික සුඛ) bodily pleasure and Kāyika dukkha (කායික දුක්ඛ) bodily pain are intended. The remaining modes of psychical Sukha (සුඛ) and dukkha (දුක්ඛ) are cētasika (චෙතසික) or mānasika (මානසික) mental pleasure and pain.

"Sukhan dukkhamupekkhanti tividhā tattha vēdanā
Sōmanassan dōmanassamitibhēdēna pancadhā
Sukhamēkattha dukkhanca dōmanassan dvayēṭṭhitan
Dvāsaṭṭhisu sōmanassan pancapaññsakētarā"

"සුඛං දුක්ඛමුපෙක්ඛන්ති තිවිධා තත්ථ වෙදනා
සොමනස්සං දොමනස්ස මිතිභෙදෙන පඤ්චධා
සුඛමෙකත්ථ දුක්ඛඤ්ච දොමනස්සං ද්වයෙට්ඨිතං
ද්වාසට්ඨීසු සොමනස්සං පඤ්චපඤ්ඤාසකෙතරා"

Pleasure, pain and neutral feeling are three aspects of sensation. They become five, when joy and sorrow are distinguished. Pleasure is one consciousness, and so is pain, grief is two. Joy sixty-two and hedonic indifference fifty-five.

FIFTY-THREE ASSOCIATED STATES

In the chapter on consciousness 89 or 121 classes of consciousness are described. One consciousness is differentiated into 89 or 121 classes according to the manner in which the 52 mental concomitants are associated with it. When all the classes are taken as one consciousness, they all have the characteristic feature of perceiving objects as in one consciousness. It is like water in several mixtures. Although water is present in several mixtures, when taken as water it is only one.

In the chapter on mental properties 52 are described. There, although contact is associated with all the 89 classes of consciousness, it should not be misunderstood as 89 contacts. Wherever contact may be present, it is only one contact which has the characteristic feature of coming in contact with an object. One particular drug appearing in several mixtures is only one; similarly, with feeling and so on. Although nescience or ignorance is associated with the twelve classes of immoral consciousness, it is only one property in that the true and real nature of the objects is not discerned. Similarly, impudence and other immoral properties. Although faith is common to all the 59 classes of morally beautiful consciousness, faith is only one according to its characteristic feature of belief in the Buddha, Dhamma and Sangha. Similarly, mindfulness and so on.

Thus, according to the characteristic feature of consciousness, it is only one, though it becomes 89 when associated with the mental properties. Contact which is obtained in the 89 associated classes, is only one according to its characteristic feature. Similarly, feeling and so on are only one and in this manner the associated states are fifty-three in number. The associated states are consciousness and mental properties.

CLASSES OF CONSCIOUSNESS OBTAINED UNDER THE SIX SUMMARIES

When the 89 classes of consciousness are analysed under feeling, as feeling is present in every consciousness, it is obtained in 89 classes.

When analysed under hētus, excepting the 18 classes unaccompanied by hētus, 71 classes are accompanied by hētus.

As every consciousness has a function to perform, function is obtained in 89.

When analysed under 'doors,' with the exception of the 19 classes of consciousness which are door-freed or outside the six doors, doors are obtained in 70 classes.

As no class of consciousness can arise without an object, object is obtained in 89 classes.

When analysed under 'bases,' the four resultant classes of consciousness in Arūpalōka and the 42 classes of consciousness that arise in Arūpalōka are obtained without a base.

FEELING

Feeling has the characteristic feature of tasting objects. Hence, its division into three, as pleasant, unpleasant and neither pleasant nor unpleasant as described in the Dhammasangini.

It has also the characteristic feature of controlling power. Hence, its division into five as pleasure, pain, joy, grief and hedonic indifference as described in Indriya Vibhanga in Vibhangappakarana. When feeling is dealt with as three-fold, bodily pleasure is included under joy and bodily pain under grief. According to this classification joy is obtained in 63 classes, grief in 3 classes and hedonic indifference in 55 classes.

In some places, feeling is described as bodily pleasure and bodily pain as two-fold. In those places neutral sensation is included under bodily pleasure, as neutral sensation is well balanced and gives a pleasurable feeling. Or neutral sensation occasioned by not doing any wrong is included under bodily pleasure, and that occasioned by doing any wrong under bodily pain. Neutral sensation occasioned by not doing any wrong is that present in moral acts as well as resultant and ineffective classes of consciousness and that occasioned by doing any wrong is what is present in immoral acts.

PAINFUL SENSATIONS

Again, the Buddha preaches in the Suttanta "Yan Kinci vēdaitamidamettha dukkhassa" (යංකිංචි වෙදයිත මිදමෙත්ථ දුක්ඛස්ස) that all sensations are painful sensations, as long as there is feeling. He states so in consideration of the fact that al! conditioned phenomena which are impermanent are ill and sorrowful. What is considered by the ignorant ones as pleasant, very pleasant, happy and so on are in reality painful by reason of their dissolution. Now, a controversy may arise as to why this feeling is described as three-fold and five-fold in Abhidhamma, and as two and one in the Sutta Pitaka. The answer is as follows :—

All feelings existing in the triple-planed universe, as they have originated depending upon some causes, are described as painful or sorrowful. Again, painful feeling is of three kinds, namely, conditioned is painful (Sankhāra dukkhan සංඛාර දුක්ඛං) changing is painful (Viparināma dukkhan විපරිනාම දුක්ඛං) and painful feeling is painful (dukkha dukkhan දුක්ඛ දුක්ඛං). Of these, birth, decay and death in the round of births, and unpleasant and painful feelings in the four planes of misery, are painful because of painful feelings therein. All other feelings, in the triple-planed universe including what is recognized as pleasant feelings, as they have originated depending on causes, are called painful because they are conditioned. One who has taken birth in the fourth Arūpalōka, known as the sphere of neither perception nor no perception, after enjoying the bliss of that Jhāna for 80,000 Maha Kappas, is obliged to change from that place and that is known as painful because of changing.

Therefore, feelings, which are conventionally known as pleasant, existing among men, Dēvās and Brahmās, as they are incapable of making any resistance against the inevitable law of dependent origination and are subject to change and come under the conditioned, they are also painful. Hence, all phenomena are included under the first Āriyan truth of ill and sorrow.

Therefore, it will be seen that description of all feeling as one of ill and sorrow is the principal preaching. Whenever it is preached as two, three or five kinds, they are secondary preachings. It should be noted that the Buddha describes the doctrine in all manner of ways according to the mentality of the audience.

HĒTUS

Of the Six conditions called Hētus.

Summarizing the Hētus, these appear as six, to wit, greed, hate, ignorance or dulness, disinterestedness, amity and intelligence[1].

NOTE 1

Amōha (අමොහ) is a synonym of paññā (පඤ්ඤා). The paññindriya cētasika (පඤ්ඤින්ද්‍රිය චෛතසික) is intended here, that is the constant element in all intellectual functioning.

Now there are eighteen kinds of consciousness which are not conditioned by any of these six :—Namely, five-door apprehending, the twice five-fold sense impressions, receiving, investigating, determining and aesthetic pleasure.

All the remaining seventy-one kinds of consciousness are conditioned by those six hētus, that is, there is one or more of the six hētus connected with them.

Of these, again, the two classes of ignorant consciousness are conditioned by one only of the hētus.

The remaining ten classes of immoral consciousness, and twelve of the Kāmalōka morally beautiful classes of consciousness, which are disconnected from knowledge, together make twenty-two kinds conditioned by two of the hētus[1].

Again, forty-seven classes of consciousness are bound up each with three[2] of the hētus, to wit, twelve classes of Kāmalōka morally beautiful consciousness which are connected with knowledge[3], and thirty-five sublime and transcendental kinds of consciousness.

NOTE 1

The eight classes rooted in greed are bound up with, or conditioned by, the two hētus, greed and ignorance ; the two classes of consciousness connected with aversion are bound up with the two hētus, hate and ignorance ; and the twelve classes of Kāmalōka morally beautiful classes disconnected from knowledge are conditioned by the two hētus disinterestedness and amity.

NOTE 2

Namely disinterestedness, amity and intelligence.

NOTE 3

That Amōha (අමොහ), of which the paññindriya cētasika (පඤ්ඤින්ද්‍රිය චේතසික) is the psychical ultimate, should be found in classes connected with knowledge shows that amōha (අමොහ), paññā (පඤ්ඤා) and ñāna (ඤාණ) refer to one and the same adjunct of consciousness.

" Lōbhō dōsōca mōhōca hētū akusalātayō
Alōbhā dōsā mōhāca kusalāvyākatā tathā
Ahētukaṭṭhārasēkahētukā dvēduvīsati
Duhētukā matā sattacattālisa tihētukā."

" ලොභො දොසොච මොහොච හෙතු අකුසලාතයො
අලොභා දොසා මොහාච කුසලා ව්‍යාකතා තථා
අහෙතුකට්ඨාරසෙකහෙතුකා ද්වෙ දුවීසති
දුහෙතුකා මතා සත්තචත්තාලිස තිහෙතුකා "

Greed, hate and ignorance are the three hētus of immoral acts.

Disinterestedness, amity and intelligence are the three hētus of moral acts and indeterminate ones as the resultants and ineffectives.

Not bound to any hētu there are 18, and bound to one hētu only there are 2, bound to two hētus there are 22, and bound to three hētus there are 47 classes of consciousness.

HOW HĒTUS ARE DIFFERENTIATED

Hētus or root conditions are of six kinds according to their characteristic features, nine kinds according to the origins of moral, immoral and indeterminate. Or, they are of twelve kinds according to the classification of moral, immoral, resultant and ineffective, and thirty-six according to the three planes of Kāmalōka, Rūpalōka and Arūpalōka.

Or, six kinds according to their characteristic features, nine according to schemata (mātikā මාතිකා), twelve according to categories, six in Kāmalōka, nine in Rūpa Arūpa and transcendental planes, three being in each. When all are taken together there are forty-two hētus or root conditions.

CLASSES OF CONSCIOUSNESS AND THEIR ROOTS

The mental property of ignorance associated with the two classes of consciousness rooted in nescience or ignorance is one unconditioned by any hētu or roots. The two classes of consciousness rooted in ignorance are conditioned by one root. The other mental concomitants associated with them are also conditioned by one root. The group of mental concomitants associated with the classes of consciousness conditioned by two roots are also conditioned by two roots. The remaining mental concomitants associated with a class of consciousness conditioned by two roots and the class of consciousness itself are consciousness and mental concomitants conditioned by two roots.

The group of mental concomitants associated with a class of consciousness conditioned by three roots are mental concomitants conditioned by three roots. The remaining concomitants and consciousness are mind and mental properties conditioned by three roots.

The roots of greed and hate are always conditioned by roots. The root of ignorance may be unconditioned by roots or conditioned by one root.

The roots of disinterestedness and amity may be conditioned by one root or two roots. The root of intelligence is always conditioned by three roots. It is, undoubtedly, a fact that there are states conditioned by three roots.

FUNCTIONS OF ROOTS

The condition of the six roots, three of which are moral and three immoral, is the ability to keep classes of consciousness conditioned by roots well established. They are similar to roots of trees which prevent their fall and keep them well established on earth.

Again, just as a tree which has taken root absorbs nutritive essence from the earth and produces flowers and fruits, even so the resulting effects, both in rebirth and during the span of life, of moral or immoral acts are occasioned by the force of the roots conditioning them.

Classes of consciousness unconditioned by roots are similar to moss on the surface of water.

ANALYSIS OF ROOTS

The three immoral hētus or roots called greed, hate and ignorance originate in the eleven planes of Kāmalōka as three.

The three moral roots of disinterestedness, amity and intelligence, originate in the eleven planes of Kāmalōka, in the fifteen planes of Rūpalōka, in the four planes of Arūpalōka and in the plane of transcendental consciousness. As three roots are obtained in each, there are twelve in these planes of existence.

Therefore, when the three immoral roots are added on to this number, there are fifteen roots in all by way of planes of existence.

As greed, hate and ignorance belong to the immoral classes, there are three immoral roots according to classes. As the three roots of disinterestedness, amity and intelligence according to schemata belong to the moral and indeterminate classes, there are six. When the three previously stated are added, they become nine. Therefore, there are nine roots according to their origin.

According to the categories of moral, immoral, resultant and ineffective, there are nine moral roots, and three immoral ones, thus becoming twelve in all.

Thus, there are six according to their characteristic features, fifteen by way of planes, nine by way of classes and twelve by way of categories. When these four groups are added, there are forty-two roots in all.

ANALYSIS OF CONSCIOUSNESS

ACCORDING TO ROOTS

Out of the 89 classes of consciousness, excluding 18 classes unconditioned by roots, the 71 classes, as they are associated with six kinds of roots, are called classes conditioned by roots.

Of these 71, the two classes of consciousness rooted in ignorance, as they are associated with only one root, are called consciousness conditioned by one root.

As, in the eight classes of consciousness rooted in greed two roots called greed and ignorance, in the two classes rooted in hate two roots called hate and ignorance, and in the twelve classes of morally beautiful consciousness disconnected from knowledge the two roots called disinterestedness and amity are associated with them, these twenty-two classes are known as consciousness conditioned by two roots.

As the twelve classes of morally beautiful consciousness connected with knowledge and the thirty-five classes of sublime and transcendental consciousness making forty-seven are associated with the three roots of disinterestedness amity and knowledge, they are called consciousness conditioned by three roots.

OF FUNCTION

FUNCTIONS

In summarizing functions, there are fourteen of these, to wit:—

(1)	Rebirth[1]	(8)	Touching
(2)	Life-continuum[2]	(9)	Receiving
(3)	Apprehending	(10)	Investigating
(4)	Seeing	(11)	Determining
(5)	Hearing	(12)	Apperceiving
(6)	Smelling	(13)	Retention[3]
(7)	Tasting	(14)	Re-decease

NOTE 1

Re-birth (paṭisandhi පටිසන්ධි) is, philosophically speaking, confined to the momentary mental function at the initial moment of reconception. In popular language, it includes reconception, embryonic growth and rebirth.

NOTE 2

Life-continuum (bhavanga භවංග) is, literally, part of existence. It is the state of mind when it does not receive external objects. In dreamless sleep we usually experience this state of mind.

NOTE 3

Retention (tadārammana තදාරම්මණ or tadālambana තදා ලම්බණ), literally, means "that object" and is the final phase in the registration of impression by way of sense. That object which has been just apperceived, if vivid enough, reaches this stage.

But if we classify these fourteen functions by way of 'stage' (ṭhāna ඨාන), then the category of stages must be considered as ten-fold[1].

NOTE 1

Ṭhāna (ඨාන), literally, place or occasion. It is pretty clear, from the fact that the only difference between (kicca කිච්ච)

function and (ṭhāna ඨාන) stage lies in five senses or a five-fold sense, that the meaning is :— The five senses having the same mental status form only one distinctive class. Only one at a time can take part in a process of presentative cognition.

Regarding consciousness under the aspect of function, we nay distinguish :—

(*a*) Nineteen classes of consciousness functioning at re-birth, during life-continuum and at re-decease, to wit :—

(i) Two classes of investigation-consciousness accompanied by hedonic indifference.

(ii) Eight classes of resultants in Kāmalōka.

(iii) Nine resultants in Rūpalōka and Arūpalōka.

(*b*) Two classes of consciousness functioning by way of the impressions called 'turning towards' the sense stimulus.

(*c*) Two classes of consciousness functioning in each of the five senses and in reception of impressions.

(*d*) Three classes of consciousness functioning by way of investigation. 'Mind-door cognition[1]' alone performs the function of determining the sense-impression at the five-doors.

(*e*) Fifty-five classes of consciousness functioning in apperception, to wit, fifty-five[2] modes of moral, immoral, fruitional and ineffective consciousness, not counting the two in (*b*).

(*f*) Eleven classes of consciousness in the retentive function, to wit, the eight great resultants and the three modes of investigation.

NOTE 1

Manōdvārāvajjana (මනොද්වාරාවජ්ජන) receives the name of votthapana (වොත්ථපන) or vottabbana (වොත්තබ්බන), when it takes part in a presentative cognition and determines the sense impression (already investigated) for apperception.

NOTE 2

Moral 21, immoral 12, fruitional 4 and ineffective 18=55.

Now, a class of consciousness may perform one or more functions :—

(i) Investigation-consciousness accompanied by hedonic indifference may perform five functions—*i.e.*, it may be active at rebirth[1], during the life-continuum, at redecease, in retention and in investigation itself.

(ii) The eight great resultants may perform four functions—*i.* e., they may be active at rebirth, during the life-continuum, at redecease and in retention.

(iii) The nine sublime classes of resultants may perform three functions—*i. e.*, they may be active at rebirth, during the life-continuum and at redecease.

(iv) Investigation-consciousness accompanied by joy may perform two functions—*i.* e., it may be active both in investigation and in retention ; and again determining consciousness may be active in determining and by way of ' turning to ' impressions.

(v) All the remaining kinds of consciousness can perform only a single function. They are the fifty-five apperceptions, the triple element of apprehension[2] and the twice five kinds of sense-cognition, each cognition functioning simply, as it comes to pass.

NOTE 1

It must not be supposed that investigation consciousness investigates its object at rebirth. This particular class of consciousness is simply active as rebirth-consciousness connecting the two consecutive existences. None of the classes of consciousness can perform more than one function at a unit of time.

NOTE 2

Manōdhātu (මනොධාතු) includes five-door cognition and the two modes of reception.

" Paṭisandhādayō nāmạ kiccabhēdēna cuddasa
Dasadhā ṭhānabhēdēna cittuppādā pakāsitā
Aṭṭhasaṭṭhi tathā dvēca navaṭṭhadvē yathākkaman
Ēkadvītucatupanca kiccaṭṭhānāni niddisē

" පටිසන්ධාදයො නාම කිච්චභෙදෙන චුද්දස
දසධාඨාන භෙදෙන චිත්තුප්පාදා පකාසිතා
අට්ඨසට්ඨි තථා ද්වෙච නවට්ඨ ද්වෙ යථාක්කමං
එකද්විතු චතු පඤ්ච කිච්චට්ඨානානි නිද්දිසෙ "

The states of consciousness, such as rebirth and so on, are fourteen according to their functions and are ten according to their stages.

Of them, one function is performed by 68 classes of consciousness, two functions by 2 classes, three functions by 9 classes, four functions by 8 classes, and five functions by 2 classes.

FUNCTIONS

The 89 classes of consciousness, described in Chapter I, perform fourteen functions. It is like 89 men employed in an industrial institution performing 14 different kinds of work. Just as a particular kind of work could be performed by a certain number of men, so could one function be performed by a certain number of classes of consciousness. Just as a man is designated by the name of the work he does, so does the class of consciousness sometimes receive the name of the function it performs. The classes of consciousness that cause rebirth are called rebirth-consciousness. In the Chapter I on consciousness, no class was described as rebirth-consciousness. Some classes of consciousness described therein perform the function of rebirth. Therefore, they are called rebirth-consciousness. The remainder should be understood in the same manner.

REBIRTH

Re-linking of one existence with another existence is the function of rebirth. Vibhavini Tīka states " bhavatō bhavassa paṭisandhānan paṭisandhi kiccan" (භවතො භවස්ස පටිසන්ධානං පටිසන්ධිකිච්චං.). Regarding one being, the flux of mind and its mental concomitants are endless. The characteristic feature of this flux or continuity is that each thought moment or unit of mental activity, which consists of three small units or time phases, to wit, nascent, static and arrested or cessant, is followed by another similar thought moment or unit of mental activity and so on. The manner in which a thought moment rises and falls is so quick and subtle that their difference is inappreciable. It is likened to a torch light being revolved round and round as fast as possible, when no space could be discerned. In this manner, the flux or continuity which consists of the rise and fall of each thought moment in one existence is broken and re-linked with another existence is the only difference. The first consciousness that originates in the second existence is known as rebirth-consciousness. It is so called because it causes the re-linking of the first existence with the second existence. The function performed by that consciousness is that of rebirth or re-linking. There are nineteen classes of consciousness that perform the function of rebirth.

LIFE-CONTINUUM

Life-continuum (bhavānga භවාඞ්ග) is explained in the Vibhavini Tīka as "avicchēdappavatti hētu bhāvēna bhavassa anga bhāvō bhavangan (අවිච්ඡේදප්පවත්ති හේතු භාවේන භවස්ස අඞ්ගභාවො භවඞ්ගං) as being the factor of life by means of which the flux or continuity of mind and its concomitants are maintained without a break. The function of life-continuum is said to be caused whenever consciousness does not perceive any sense impression through the five-doors or conceive of an idea or concept through the mind-door. It is likened to a spider that remains stationary in the middle of a web consisting of many threads. When an insect alights on any thread, the spider instantaneously runs in that direction to get hold of the insect, and at other times remains stationary. That the life-continuum is similar to this should be understood. The consciousness of life-continuum too perceives objects, which are free from doors.

The objects that are free from doors are Kamma, sign of Kamma, and sign of destiny resembling that which occasioned rebirth by way of plane, class, associated states, volitional activities and objects. Life-continuum in the absence of any process of cognition goes on in an unbroken flux like the stream of a river or a flame of a lamp. There are 19 classes of consciousness that perform the function of life-continuum.

APPREHENDING

The functions of apprehending are two, namely, five-door apprehending and mind-door apprehending. The function of apprehending is turning to or directing its attention to presentative as well as representative objects. It is likened to a spider that turns to or directs its attention to ascertain in what direction that which caused the vibration of its body came from, on an insect alighting on its web.

SEEING

The function of seeing is performed by the two classes of visual consciousness that perceive pleasant and unpleasant objects.

HEARING

The function of hearing is performed by the two classes of auditory consciousness that hear pleasant and unpleasant sounds.

SMELLING

The function of smelling is performed by the two classes of olfactory consciousness that smell pleasant and unpleasant odours.

TASTING

The function of tasting is performed by the two classes of gustatory consciousness that taste sapids.

TOUCHING

The function of touching is performed by the two classes of tactile consciousness that feel bodily pleasure and bodily pain.

RECEIVING

The function of receiving is performed by the two classes of consciousness that receive sense impressions which have come within the avenue of the five-doors.

INVESTIGATING

The function of investigating is performed by three classes of consciousness that investigate the sense impressions already received.

DETERMINING

The function of determining is performed by one class of consciousness that determines the sense impressions already investigated. This is a particular variety of apprehending.

APPERCEIVING

The function of apperceiving is performed by fifty-five classes of consciousness which after determining an object cause moral or immoral acts in running succession, ordinarily seven states of consciousness in a process of thought through any of the five doors, and three times seven through the mind door before the act is completed.

RETENTION

The function of retention is performed by eleven classes of consciousness which retain the object that has been apperceived.

RE-DECEASE

The function of re-decease is performed by nineteen classes of consciousness which cause the passing off of the flux or continuity of mind and its concomitants in one existence. The functions of rebirth, life-continuum and re-decease are performed by one class of consciousness. When rebirth has been occasioned by a particular class of consciousness, the same class is present in the life-continuum when no sense impressions are perceived by the doors, and at the end of existence becomes re-decease consciousness.

STAGES OR PLACES

In order that the functions, such as rebirth and so on, may be better understood their stages or places will now be described. When two boundaries are shown the middle could be understood easily. The stages or places are as follows :—

(1)	Stage of rebirth	(6)	Stage of investigating
(2)	do life-continuum	(7)	do determining
(3)	do apprehending	(8)	do apperceiving
(4)	do five cognitions	(9)	do retention
(5)	do receiving	(10)	do re-decease

Stages are places where the classes of consciousness arise. By calling them stages, it should not be misunderstood that different classes of consciousness perform the functions other than those of stages.

1. Stage of rebirth is the place where the classes of consciousness, which give rise to rebirth, arise. It is between re-decease and the life-continuum. Re-decease immediately precedes rebirth, and life-continuum immediately follows it. It is natural for a sequence of life-continuum to take place immediately following rebirth.

2. Stage of life-continuum is the place where the series of life-continuum arise. They are between rebirth and the two apprehending, between apperception and the two apprehending, between retention and the two apprehending, between determining and the two apprehending, at times between apperceptions and re-decease, and between retention and re-decease.

Immediately following rebirth is the life-continuum, and immediately following the life-continuum one of the two apprehending. Therefore, the life-continuum is between the rebirth and the two apprehending.

3. Stage of apprehending is the place where the two classes of apprehending arise. The apprehending are five-door apprehending and mind-door apprehending. Five-door apprehending is between the life-continuum and the five-fold cognition. Mind-door is between the life-continuum and apperceptions.

4. Five-fold cognition is the place where the two classes of visual cognition, the two classes of auditory cognition, the two classes of olfactory, the two of gustatory, and the two of tactile cognitions arise. They arise in each process of thought through the five-doors between the five-door apprehending and the two receiving classes of consciousness.

5. Stage of receiving is the place where the two classes of receiving consciousness arise. They are between the five-fold cognition and the investigating classes of consciousness. Immediately following the five-fold cognition is the receiving and following the receiving, the investigating arise. Therefore, receiving is between the five-fold cognition and investigating.

6. Stage of investigating is the place where investigating classes of consciousness arise. They are between the receiving and the determining. Investigating immediately follows receiving and immediately following the investigating is the determining in five door process of thought.

7. Stage of determining is the place where consciousness of determining arises. Mind-door itself performs the function of determining in a five-door process of thought. This arises between the investigating and the apperceiving, and between the investigating and the life-continuum.

8. Stage of apperceiving is the place where the fifty-five classes of consciousness performing the function of apperceiving arise. They arise between determining and retention, between determining and life-continua, between determining and re-decease, between mind-door apprehending and retention, between mind-door apprehending and the life-continua and between the mind-door apprehending and re-decease.

9. Stage of retention is the place where the eleven classes of consciousness performing the function of retention arise. They arise between the apperceiving and the life-continua, between the apperceiving and re-decease. Immediately following the apperceiving retention arises, and immediately following retention life-continuum arises. Therefore, retention is between the apperceiving and life-continuum. Similarly, sometimes retention immediately follows the apperceiving and re-decease

immediately follows retention. Then retention takes place between the apperceiving and re-decease.

10. Stage of re-decease is the place where the 19 classes of consciousness that perform the function of re-decease arise. They arise between the apperceiving and rebirth, between retention and rebirth and between the life-continuum and rebirth. Sometimes re-decease immediately follows the apperceiving, sometimes immediately after retention re-decease occurs, and sometimes becoming life-continuum redecease sets in.

TWENTY-FIVE STAGES

From the above description it should be noted that there are 25 stages in all viz: 1 stage of rebirth, 6 stages of life-continuum, 2 of apprehending, 1 of five-fold cognition, 1 of receiving, 1 of investigation, 2 of determining, 6 of apperceiving, 2 of retention and 3 of re-decease.

The stage of rebirth could be understood from the process of thought at the time of death.

The 6 stages of life-continuum, when the two processes of thought at the time of death, one stage of rebirth, during the span of life one process of thought in which the intensity of the object is very great, one process of thought in which the intensity of the object is small, and one in which the intensity of the object is very small, are all taken together, could be understood.

The 2 stages of apprehending are one in a five-door process of thought and one in a mind-door process of thought.

The five-fold cognition, receiving and investigating stages are obtained in a five-door process of thought.

The two stages of determining occur in one place in the two processes of thought in which the intensity of object is very great and in one place in the process of thought in which the intensity of the object is small.

The six stages of apperceiving are (1) process of thought with a very intense object (2) process of thought with an intense object (3) mind-door process with a clear object (4) mind-door process with an obscure object (5) minor-door process at the time of death causing re-decease and following the apperceiving and (6) five-door process at the time of death causing re-decease and following the apperceiving.

The 3 stages of retention are two arising during the span of life and one at the time of death.

The 3 stages of re-decease are the three that arise at the three thought processes at the time of birth.

CLASSES OF CONSCIOUSNESS PERFORMING THE FUNCTION OF REBIRTH

1. There are 19 classes of consciousness performing the function of rebirth. They are as follows :—

(*a*) Two classes of investigating consciousness accompanied by hedonic indifference.
(*b*) Eight great resultants.
(*c*) Five resultants of Rūpalōka.
(*d*) Four resultants of Arūpalōka.

The two classes of investigating consciousness accompanied by hedonic indifference are the immoral resultant and the moral resultant unconditioned by hētus or roots.

2. Of the twelve classes of immoral consciousness, with the exception of the class accompanied by indifference and conjoined with distraction, the remaining eleven will have resulting effects by way of rebirth. As rebirth resultant in any of the four planes of misery, it is the immoral resultant called investigating consciousness accompanied by indifference that occurs immediately after re-decease. It is this consciousness that performs the function of rebirth. Without the intervention of a Dēva or Brahma, but solely by the force of immoral consciousness the doer of the immoral act is born in a plane of misery, and that is certain. It is the same in other places too.

3. Out of the eight moral classes of consciousness in Kāmalōka, the rebirth resultant of weak moral consciousness conditioned

by two roots is the moral resultant of investigating accompanied by hedonic indifference. It causes birth in the world of men with eyes blind or defective sensory organs and so on. The weak moral consciousness conditioned by two roots are the four classes of moral consciousness disconnected from knowledge which are not obtained alike during the three periods, namely, before the performance of the act, during the act and after the act.

4. The eight great resultants are the eight classes of resultant consciousness conditioned by roots. How they arise by way of rebirth will be briefly stated here. The four resultant classes of consciousness conditioned by three roots obtained from moral consciousness of a very high order and conditioned by three roots arise by way of rebirth. Moral consciousness conditioned by three roots becomes of a very high order, when the four classes of moral consciousness in Kāmalōka connected with knowledge are obtained alike before the act, during the act and after the act. The four classes of resultant consciousness conditioned by three roots are the four connected with knowledge.

5. Weak moral consciousness conditioned by three roots as well as moral consciousness of a very high order and conditioned by two roots give rise to four resultant classes of consciousness conditioned by two roots by way of rebirth. Moral consciousness conditioned by three roots becomes weak, when the four classes of moral consciousness connected with knowledge take place only during the act and neither before nor after the act. Or, it may be that during the act it is connected with knowledge and after the act disconnected from knowledge. The resultants conditioned by two roots, are the four resultants disconnected from knowledge.

6. How weak moral consciousness conditioned by two roots gives rise to resultants unconditioned by roots was described before under para (3).

7. The five resultants in Rūpalōka are obtained by way of effects from the corresponding five classes of moral consciousness in Rūpalōka.

8. The four resultants in Arūpalōka are obtained by way of effects from the corresponding four classes of moral consciousness in Arūpalōka.

OF DOORS (OR ORGANS)

In the summary of doors, door is the name given to six organs, to wit :—eye-door, ear-door, nose-door, tongue-door, body-door and mind-door.

Here the eye is just the eye-door ; and so for the ear-door and the next three. But the life-continuum may be described as the mind-door.

Of these organs, through the first, the door of sight, forty-six classes of consciousness take their rise according to fitness in subject and object[1], to wit :—(*a*) five-door cognition (*b*) visual cognition (*c*) reception (*d*) investigating (*e*) determining (*f*) Kāmalōka apperception and (*g*) retention.

So for the next four 'doors' as auditory cognition and so on. And when all are reckoned, there are fifty-four kinds of Kāmalōka consciousness which take their rise through the five 'doors.'

NOTE 1

Abhidhammattha Vibhāvini explains the yathārahan (යථාරහං) as follows :—According as the object is agreeable or not ; as that object is properly attended to or not ; and as the percipient is an Arahant or not etc. Ledi Sadaw explains the same by 'according to the object the plane of existence, the subject attention' etc.

But, by way of the mind-door, sixty-seven kinds of consciousness come to pass to wit, mind-door consciousness, the fifty-five kinds of apperception and retention.

There are nineteen kinds of consciousness which are free, in functioning from any door ; namely, those which are active at rebirth, during the life-continuum and at re-decease.

Of those, on the other hand, which take their rise through doors, thirty-six kinds of consciousness come to pass through one door, according as there is mutual fitness, to wit, the twice five classes of sense-consciousness, sublime and transcendental apperceptions.

The triple element of apprehension comes to pass through five-doors.

Investigating accompanied by pleasure, determining consciousness and Kāmalōka apperceptions are cognitions happening through six-doors.

Investigating which is accompanied by hedonic indifference and the great resultant classes of consciousness happen either by way of the six-doors or are independent of any door[1].

Resultant sublime cognitions are always independent of any door.

NOTE 1

According to the commentators, the former is the case in our investigating and retaining ; the latter, at rebirth, during unconscious life and at re-decease.

" Ēkadvārika cittāni panca chadvārikānica
Chadvārika vimuttāni vimuttānica sabbathā
Chattinsati tathā tīni ēkatinsa yathākkaman
Dasadhā navadhācēti pancadhā parideepayē "

" එකද්වාරික චිත්තානි පඤ්ච ඡද්වාරිකානි ච
ඡද්වාරික විමුත්තානි විමුත්තානි ච සබ්බථා
ඡත්තිංසති තථා තීණි එකතිංස යථාක්කමං
දසධා නවධාචෙති පඤ්චධා පරිදීපයෙ "

There are 36 classes of consciousness arising through one door, 3 through the five-doors, 31 through six-doors, 1c through the six doors and door-freed and 9 door-freed. Thus, in this summary five heads of difference are shown.

SUMMARY OF DOORS

Doors are ordinarily used for the entrance and exit of people. Here, through the eye-door 46 classes of consciousness gain entrance when a visual object comes in contact with it, and make their exit from the same door. The arising of consciousness is similar to the entrance, and its ceasing is similar to the exit. Therefore, it is called eye-door. In the four doors known as ear-door, nose-door, tongue-door and body-door, when sound, smell, sapids and touch come in contact, forty-six classes of consciousness arise and cease through each of those four doors.

EYE-DOOR

By eye is meant the sensitive element of the eye, or that material quality in the eye, capable of seeing visual objects. When the eye itself becomes a door, it is known as eye-door. According to Vibhāvini Tika, the material eye itself is called the eye and, according to Manisaramanjusa, the nine material qualities, excluding the sensitive material quality of the eye, out of the group of " eye-decad " are called the eye.

EAR-DOOR

By ear is meant the sensitive element of the ear, or that material quality in the internal ear, capable of hearing auditory objects. When the ear itself becomes a door, it is known as ear door.

NOSE-DOOR

By nose is meant the sensitive element of the nose, or that material quality inside the nose resembling a goat's hoof, capable of smelling odours. When the nose itself becomes a door, it is known as nose-door.

TONGUE-DOOR

By tongue is meant the sensitive element of the tongue, or material quality present in the tongue, capable of tasting sapids. When the tongue itself becomes a door, it is known as tongue-door.

BODY-DOOR

By body is meant the sensitive element of the body, or the material quality of the body present all over the body, with the exception of the ends of hair, nails, down and dried epithelial scales, capable of perceiving touch. When the body itself becomes a door, it is known as body-door.

MIND-DOOR

By mind is meant the life-continuum. It is not the ordinary life-continuum, but the life-continuum that gets arrested immediately before the consciousness that turns to sense impressions. When the mind itself becomes a door, it is known as mind-door.

If such be the case, a question may be asked as to whether each of the life-continua immediately following rebirth consciousness, which also gets arrested before the arising of the succeeding one, is also called the mind-door. They should not be considered as mind-doors, for, from the first life-continuum up to the last one in the series, each gets arrested for the origination of the immediately contiguous ones. It is only the life-continuum that gets arrested for the origination of a thought process is called the mind-door.

If such be the case, would the life continuum that gets arrested for the origination of a five-door process of thought, whenever a sense impression comes in contact with any of the doors as eye and so on, be called the mind-door? The reply to that question is in the negative. The life-continuum that gets arrested for the origination of the five-door apprehending is common to all the five doors and not to a particular door. Therefore, it is only the life-continuum that gets arrested before the origination of the mind-door apprehending that is called the mind-door.

ILLUSTRATION

The life-continuum that gets arrested before the origination of the five-door apprehending and the mind-door apprehending could be understood by the following illustration :—On a very cloudy day, without any sunshine, when a bird alights on the end of a branch of a tree, its image does not fall on the ground. Similarly, the life-continuum that gets arrested immediately before the arising of the five-door apprehending. Whereas, on the other hand, on a bright sunny day, when a bird alights on the end of a branch of a tree, then that act and the falling of the shadow of the bird take place simultaneously without any appreciable interval of time. Similarly, the life-continuum that gets arrested immediately before the origination of the mind-door apprehending, and objects or concepts coming in contact with the mind-door apprehending cognition take place simultaneously.

CLASSES OF CONSCIOUSNESS THROUGH THE EYE-DOOR

The 46 classes of consciousness arising through the eye-door are as follows :—

(1) Five-door apprehending
(2) Two classes of visual cognition
(3) Two classes of recipient consciousness
(4) Three classes of investigating consciousness
(5) One class of determining consciousness
(6) Twenty-nine classes of Kāmalōka apperceptions, viz. 12 immoral, 1 of aesthetic pleasure (ineffective), 8 morally beautiful and 8 ineffective classes conditioned by roots.
(7) Eight classes of retention, which are the great resultants conditioned by roots

Although the three classes of investigating consciousness are also classes of retention they are not included under (7) as they have already been counted under retention class.

These classes would be better understood when processes of thought are studied later.

CLASSES OF CONSCIOUSNESS THROUGH THE OTHER FOUR DOORS

The number of classes of consciousness arising through each of the other four doors is the same. The difference would be the substitution of the corresponding classes of consciousness, such as the two auditory consciousness and so on, in place of visual consciousness.

Therefore, it will be seen that there are 54 classes of consciousness through the five doors.

CLASSES OF CONSCIOUSNESS THROUGH THE MIND-DOOR

There are 67 classes of consciousness arising through the mind-door viz :—

(1) One class of mind-door apprehending
(2) 55 classes of apperceptions
(3) 11 classes of retention.

Here, as the three classes of investigation are also included, the retention classes become eleven.

CLASSES OF CONSCIOUSNESS THAT ARE DOOR-FREED

There are 19 classes of consciousness which do not arise through any of the six doors, but perform the functions of rebirth, life-continuum and redecease. Therefore, they are called 'door-freed.' They are as follows :—

(1) 2 classes of resultant consciousness unconditioned by roots called investigating consciousness, one resulting from immoral deeds done in a previous birth, and the other from moral deeds done in a previous birth.
(2) Eight great classes of Kāmalōka resultants
(3) Five resultants of Rūpalōka
(4) Four resultants of Arūpalōka.

OF OBJECT OF CONSCIOUSNESS

In the summary of objects, that which is called object is of six kinds, to wit :—visible object, audible object, odorous object, sapid object, tangible object and cognizable object. Here, only one visible form is visible object; again, only sound is audible object and so forth.

NOTE 1

Rūpa (රූප) here seems to be confined to the vannāyatana (වණ්ණායතන), or sense of colour, the only strictly visible object (sanidassana rūpan සනිදස්සන රූපං), the form, the figure, the shape (sanṭhāna සණ්ඨාන) being known inferentially in any one of the sequels of sense cognition.

But cognizable object is classified under six groups, to wit, the sensitive parts of the organs, subtle forms[1], cognitions, mental concomitants, Nibbāna and name-and-notion[2].

Here, of all cognitions arising through the organ of sight, visible form is the object and such visible form as is present. Again, of all cognitions arising through the organs of hearing, smell, taste and touch, the corresponding sense objects only are the objects, and they are present objects.

NOTE 1

'Gross' and 'subtle' is one division of all rūpa (රූප) or non-mental forms (*i.e.* material qualities). The former comprises all sense-organs and sense-objects; the latter, the principles or states of the two sexes, the vital principle, the two media of communication (viññatti විඤ්ඤත්ති), space, certain properties of matter and the nutritive principles in foods.

NOTE 2

Paññatti (පඤ්ඤත්ති) includes nāma paññatti (name or term) and attha paññatti (notion, idea or concept).

But the object of mind-door cognition is a sixfold present, past or future object, or one out of time, according to its capacities.

Further, the objects of those 'door-freed' classes of consciousness which are called rebirth, life-continuum and re-decease cognitions, are also of six kinds according to circumstances. They have usually been grasped in the immediately preceding existence by way of the six doors[1]; they are objects of things either present, or past or they are concepts[2]. And they are known as Karma, sign of Karma or sign of destiny[3].

NOTE 1

And that at the time of approaching death.

NOTE 2

The attha paññatti (අත්ථපඤ්ඤත්ති) is here intended, that is, the idea, the notion or the conecpt.

NOTE 3

Gatinimittan (ගතිනිමිත්තං), literally, 'sign of going' or of the objective of one's going, that is, of one's destiny.

Of those classes of consciousness which have this or that object, visual cognition has visible form only as its object; similarly, in the case of the other four senses. But the objects of the triple element of apprehension[1] are five-fold, being the five sense-objects.

The remaining kinds of Kāmalōka resultant consciousness, as well as aesthetic pleasure,, have in all cases only Kāmalōka objects.

Immoral consciousness, as well as such Kāmalōka apperceptions as are disconnected from knowledge, may have all kinds of objects except transcendental objects[2].

NOTE 1

Triple element of apprehension is manōdhātuttikan (මනොධාතුත්තිකං), that is, five-door apprehending and the two classes of recipient consciousness.

NOTE 2

The commentators number these as nine, the four Paths, the four Fruits and Nibbāna.

Those classes of Kāmalōka moral consciousness which are connected with knowledge, as well as those belonging to super-intellection which is reckoned as of fifth Jhāna moral consciousness, may have all kinds of objects except the Path and Fruit of Arahantship.

Ineffective Kāmalōka consciousness which is connected with knowledge, as well as ineffective super-intellection and determining cognition, may have all kinds of objects under any conditions.

In purely Arūpalōka consciousness, the second and the fourth class have only sublime objects[1]. All the remaining kinds of sublime consciousness have objects which are concepts[2].

Transcendental consciousness has Nibbāna as its object.

Note 1

The sublime objects are the first and the third Āruppas (Arūpalōka Jhānas.)

Note 2

Paññattālambanāni (පඤ්ඤත්තාලම්බනානි) Atthapaññatti (අත්ථපඤ්ඤත්ති) is here intended. All the five stages of Jhāna in the fifteen classes of Rūpalōka consciousness are induced by the paṭibhāga nimitta (පටිභාගනිමිත්ත) or the transformed after-image (*i.e.* the image conceptualized) of one or other of the ten Kasina circles, or by the after image arising in the breathing exercise. But the after image of any of the ten impurities or of the living body is capable of inducing the first stage only of the Jhāna. The first four stages of Jhāna induced by the exercise of amity, pity and appreciation are worked on the concept 'mankind' ; but the fifth stage induced by 'equanimity' is also concerned with that concept not as an object of amity, pity or appreciation, but as an object of relative indifference. The first exercise in the Arūpa Jhāna is on the concept 'space' ; the third Arūpa Jhāna is exercised on the concept 'nothingness.' Thus, the fifteen Rūpa and the six Arūpa Jhānas twenty-one in all, work by concepts.

" Pancaveesa parittamhi cha cittāni mahaggatē
Ēkaveesati vōhāre aṭṭha nibbāna gōcharē
Veesānuttara muttamhi agga magga phalujjitē
panca sabbattha chaccēti sattadhā tattha sangaho."

" පච‌වීස පරිත්තම්හි ඡ චිත්තානි මහග්ගතෙ
එකවීසති වොහාරෙ අට්ඨ නිබ්බාන ගොචරෙ
වීසානුත්තර මුත්තම්හි අග්ග මග්ග ඵලුජ්ජිතෙ
පච සබ්බත්ථ ඡච්චෙති සත්තධා තත්ථ සංගහො"

The 23 classes of Kāmalōka resultants, five-door apprehending and the ineffective class of aesthetic pleasure, in all 25 classes, have for their objects only the Kāmalōka ones.

6 classes, namely, the 3 moral, resultant and ineffective classes of the 2nd Arūpa Jhāna dwelling on the infinity of consciousness and the 3 moral, resultant and ineffective classes of the 4th

Arūpa Jhāna, dwelling on the infinity of neither perception nor no perception, have for their objects sublime ones, namely, those of Rūpalōka and Arūpalōka.

15 classes of Rūpalōka consciousness and 6 classes of Arūpalōka consciousness belonging to the first and third Jhānas, making 21 in all, have for their objects concepts, that is, transformed after-image, obtained from Kasina circles.

The 8 classes of transcendental consciousness have for their object Nibbāna.

The 12 classes of immoral consciousness and the 8 classes of moral and ineffective disconnected from knowledge, making 20 in all, have for their objects all others excepting the transcendental.

The 4 classes of moral consciousness connected with knowledge, and the moral consciousness of super-intellection, in all five, have for their objects, all others excepting, the Path and Fruit of Arahatship.

The 4 classes of ineffective consciousness connected with knowledge, the ineffective consciousness of super-intellection and the mind-door apprehending, six in all, have for their objects all kinds of objects.

In the summary of objects seven kinds of objects are taken by different kinds of consciousness.

OBJECTS

Consciousness is like a weak person. A weak person is unable to stand without a support. Similarly, consciousness cannot arise spontaneously without the support of an object. Any phenomena which are helpful for the origination of consciousness are called objects (ālambana ආලම්බන). These ālambana (ආලම්බන) are also called ārammana (ආරම්මන), because the states of consciousness that arise through the eye-door and so on receive support from them by contact.

There are six kinds of objects, viz. visual object, auditory object, odorous object, sapid object, tangible object and cognizable object.

VISUAL OBJECT

The sense of colour such as blue, yellow and so on, and their appearance such as long or short, square or octagonal, are called visual objects because their impression is perceived by the eye. The 46 classes of consciousness arising through the eye-door take for their object only the present visual object. Here, present is of three kinds, namely,

(1) Present meaning moment (Khana paccuppanna ඛණ පච්චුප්පන්න)
(2) Present meaning continuity (santati paccuppanna සන්තති පච්චුප්පන්න) and
(3) Present meaning by way of duration (addhā paccuppanna අද්ධා පච්චුප්පන්න).

Of these, present moment of an object is that which lasts for seventeen thought moments, as such is the duration of life of the present object.

When any object is seen by the eye, one process of thought through the eye-door and three reproductive sequels through the mind-door take place, after which the impression of the visual object is perceived. The duration of time taken by these four processes of thought is called the continuous present.

The duration of time from the rebirth consciousness up to redecease consciousness, whether it is hundred years or a little more or less, that is, the span of life in one existence, is called the present by way of duration.

Of these three kinds of present, it should be understood that the present visual object referred to is the present moment, that is, that object which lasts for seventeen thought moments only, after which the object ceases.

Similarly, in respect of audible, odorous, sapid and tangible objects, the present moment should be understood as that object which lasts for seventeen thought moments before its cessation.

AUDIBLE OBJECTS

The 46 classes of consciousness arising through the ear-door have for their object only the present audible objects, that is, sounds of words spoken, laughter and so on, sounds caused by drums and so on, the duration of which is only seventeen thought moments.

ODOROUS OBJECTS

The 46 classes of consciousness arising through the nose-door have for their object only the present odorous objects such as incense, camphor, perfumes and so on. Here too, by present is meant that object which lasts for only seventeen thought moments.

SAPID OBJECTS

The 46 classes of consciousness arising through the tongue-door have also for their object sapids such as sweet, acid, saltish, bitter, hot and so on, which is momentarily present, the life term of which is only seventeen thought moments.

TANGIBLE OBJECTS

The 46 classes of consciousness arising through the body-door have for their objects tangible objects originated by kamma as well as those not originated by kamma. In any case the tangible object consists of the elements of extension, heat or cold and motion, and not that of cohesion. Here too, only the tangible object, which lasts for seventeen thought moments, is the present object.

COGNIZABLE OBJECTS

The cognizable objects are of six kinds, to wit :—(1) sensitive material qualities derived from the four great essentials (2) subtle material qualities, (3) mind, (4) mental concomitants, (5) Nibbāna, (6) concept, idea or notion, as well as name or term.

1. The sensitive material qualities of the eye, ear, nose, tongue and body are the controlling powers of sense organs.

2. The subtle material qualities are the element of cohesion, material qualities of sex, female and male, material quality of the heart-base, the vital power, material quality of food or

nutritive essence, material quality of space, the two media of communication by body and speech, the three material qualities of plasticity, viz. those of buoyancy, pliancy and adaptability and the four material qualities of marks viz. integration, continuity, decay and impermanence.

3. Mind is 89 or 121 classes of consciousness.

4. Mental concomitants are the 52 properties such as contact and so on.

5. Nibbāna is the unconditioned state that is intuited by the four Paths and four Fruits.

6. Paññatti is what is conventionally known as mountain, rock, house, Kasina circle and so on, that is, a name or a term (nāma paññatti) or a concept, idea or a notion (attha paññatti).

Of these Nibbāna and Paññatti are ree from time, because they are never extinguished and because they cannot be differentiated into past, present and future. All others belong to the past, present and future.

The 67 classes of consciousness arising through the mind-door have for their objects, either past or present or future, the five sensory objects such as visual object and so on, also the sensitive material qualities of the sense organs, subtle material qualities, mind and mental concomitants and time-freed Nibbāna and Paññatti (name or term) according to circumstances, that is, according as they are Kāmalōka apperceptions, super-intellection apperceptions, and the other sublime apperceptions.

Kāmalōka apperceptions, with the exception of the ineffective class of aesthetic pleasure, have for their objects, either present past or future, the six sensory objects such as visual object and so on, and the time freed Nibbāna and name or term.

The class of aesthetic pleasure has for its objects the past, future and present visual objects and so on. That is because it belongs to Kāmalōka consciousness.

Super-intellection apperceptions which arise by way of celestial eye and so on have for their objects, according to circumstances, the five sensory objects during the three periods of time, and Nibbāṇa and name or term free from time. For instance, celestial eye has for its objects the present visual object, and the celestial ear the present audible object. But the powers of Iddhi have for their objects the six sensory objects such as visual object and so on during the three periods of time. The super-intellection by which others' thoughts are discerned has for its object both past and future cognizable objects. Super-intellection remembering past births has for its objects only the past six kinds of sensory objects such as visual object and so on, and those free from time.

OF BASES

In the summary of bases, what are called 'bases' are of six kinds, to wit, the bases : eye, ear, nose, tongue, body and heart.

In Kāmalōka all these obtain. In the world of Rūpa there exists no base of smell, taste or touch. In the world of Arūpa none of the bases exists.

Now the five elements of sense-cognition proceed wholly and solely in dependence of the five sensory organs as their respective bases. But the elements of mind—that is to say, adverting, and reception of the five door impressions, proceed solely in dependence of the heart; the element of mind-consciousness[1], comprising investigating-cognitions, the main classes of resultant consciousness, the two 'aversive' kinds of consciousness, the consciousness of the first Path, aesthetic pleasure and Rūpalōka consciousness, proceed in dependence of the heart.

But all other classes of consciousness, when they are moral or immoral, ineffective or transcendental, are either dependent on, or independent of, the heart base. When they are Arūpalōka resultants, they are independent of the heart base.

NOTE 1

Manōviññāna dhātu (මනෝ විඤ්ඤාණ ධාතු), literally rendered so as to cover the seventy-six classes of consciousness named, which are capable of taking part in both presentative and representative cognition. It may be called the element of comprehension to distinguish it from the element of apprehension (manōdhātu මනොධාතු).

" Chavatthu nissitā kāmē satta rūpē catubbidhā
Tivatthu nissitā ruppē dhātvēkā nissitā matā
Tēcattālisa nissāya dvēcattālisa jāyarē
Nissāyaca anissāya pākāruppā anissitāti."

"ඡවත්ථු නිස්සිතා කාමෙ සත්ත රූපෙ චතුබ්බිධා
තිවත්ථු නිස්සිතා රූප්පෙ ධාතෙවකා නිස්සිතාමතා
තෙ චත්තාලිස නිස්සාය ද්වෙ චත්තාලිස ජායරෙ
නිස්සායච අනිස්සාය පාකාරූප්පා අනිස්සිතාති"

In Kāmalōka the seven elements of cognition exist in dependence of the six bases of eye and so on.

In Rūpalōka the element of eye cognition, the element of ear cognition, the element of mind and the element of mind-consciousness exist in dependence of the three bases of eye, ear and heart.

In Arūpalōka the only element of mind-consciousness exists without the six bases, that is to say, that it has no base at all.

Forty-three classes of consciousness exist in dependence of the six bases. They are 23 Kāmalōka resultants, five-door apprehending, aesthetic pleasure, the two aversives, 15 Rūpalōka classes and the transcendental consciousness belonging to the first Path.

Forty-two classes of consciousness exist in dependence of, or independent of, the heart-base. They exist in dependence of the heart-base in Kāmalōka and Rūpalōka where the five aggregates exist, and independent of the heart-base in Arūpalōka where only the mind and mental concomitants, or only four aggregates, exist.

SIX BASES

There are six bases, to wit, eye-base, ear-base, nose-base, tongue-base, body-base and heart-base. Base is the place where the mind and mental concomitants arise. Sometimes they arise in the eye and so on. When a visual object comes in contact with the sensitive material quality of the eye, consciousness existing in the heart-base vibrates, gets arrested, apprehends through the five doors and perceives an impression of a visual object, which is called eye-cognition. Because the consciousness of eye-cognition arises in the eye or in dependence of the eye, the eye is called the eye-base.

Similarly, ear-base and so on. But, the heart-base is a material quality originated from Kamma and associated with the blood in the heart, where the element of mind and the element of mind-consciousness arise. Because they arise in the heart or in dependence of the heart, the heart is called the heart-base.

HEART AND ITS BASE

The heart is situated in the chest cavity between the two breasts and more inclined to the left assuming a shape resembling a lotus bud with its apex turned downwards. The interior of the heart is not smooth but elevated and depressed in such a way as to resemble the external surface of the vegetable called 'Vatakolu' (වැටකොලු). The heart-base, which is a material quality derived from the four great essentials and originated from Kamma, is associated with the blood contained in the heart cavity. The element of mind (five-door apprehending and pair of recipient consciousness) and the element of mind-consciousness, (76 classes of consciousness) that is to say, the element of apprehension and comprehension exist depending on the heart-base.

HEART AND ITS CONTENTS

The heart is said to be small in the case of intelligent people and large in the ignorant, and the heart cavity large in the intelligent and small in the ignorant. The blood in the heart cavity becomes jet black like a very ripe 'Dan' (දං ඇට) fruit, when one gets very angry. At a time when there is lust and greed of great intensity, the blood assumes the colour of water resulting from washing meat. When the ignorance is very great, it becomes the colour of water resulting from washing rice. The blood of one with an imaginative temperament is like the colour of the water resulting from boiling 'Kollu' (කොල්ලු) beans. The blood of one with a devotional temperament is sparkling and resembles either the colour of pearls or yellow like the colour of 'Kinihiri' (කිණිහිරි) flowers. The blood of an intelligent person is red resembling the colour of rubies.

NUMBER OF BASES EXISTING IN DIFFERENT PLANES

All the six bases exist in beings born in Kāmalōka, whose sensory organs are not defective in any way.

In Rūpalōka, with the exception of the sphere of unconscious beings, nose-base, tongue-base and body-base are absent. How is it that the eye-base and ear-base exist and not the other three? By reason of the presence of the eye-base and ear-base, moral classes of consciousness can arise by seeing the Buddha and hearing the doctrine. By means of the nose, tongue and body, one is able to gratify one's senses through those organs, but they would not help one to accumulate good Kamma. Therefore, the three bases of nose, tongue and body are not present in the 15 spheres of Brahmalōka. Again, having realized the futility and the danger of indulging in sense desires, by mental culture and concentration one detaches oneself from sensuous pleasure and attenuates the craving for them, and after cultivating Jhānas he is born in Rūpalōka without the three bases of nose, tongue and body. This does not mean that they are devoid of the ordinary nose, tongue and body.

In the sphere of unconscious beings, there is not a single base present but only a physical body.

In Arūpalōka the aggregate of rūpa (material qualities) is totally absent, but the mind and mental concomitants exist, not depending on the heart-base.

CONTROVERSY RE HEART-BASE

With regard to the heart-base, there is a conflict of opinion as to whether it is in the heart or the brain, or in both, or anywhere else in the human system. Criticism is also levelled against the commentators that, when the Buddha never stated the organ in which it existed, they erroneously expounded that it was present in the heart.

The Buddha states " Yan rūpan nissāya manōdhātuca manō viññāna dhātuca pavattantin rūpan (යං රූපං නිසසාය මනො ධාතුව මනොවිඤඤාණ ධාතුව පවතතනතිං රූපං) that in dependence of a material quality the element of mind and the element of mind-consciousness exist and that material quality is referred to by him. Because the Buddha does not specify in which organ this material quality exists, whether in the heart, or brain, or both, or anywhere else in the human system, it is illogical and unreasonable to challenge the exposition of the commentators and accuse them by alleging that they state that it is the heart. What the commentators do state is that this material quality of heart-base, which is derived from the four great essentials and originated from Kamma, is associated with the blood in the heart organ. As the blood is circulated all over the body and is a product of the heart, the commentators are quite justifiable in designating this material quality as heart-base, and not as a brain-base, although there is an inter-relation between the heart and the brain in that the heart cannot perform its functions without the necessary innervation from the brain, nor could the brain perform its functions without the necessary blood supply from the heart. That the heart is the more important of the two could be deduced from the fact that death is more often caused by stoppage of heart's action than from other causes. That it is not located in the brain could be understood easily by the fact that consciousness may arise anywhere in the body under necessary circumstances, for blood which is pumped out by the heart supplies the whole body.

The Scientists and western Philosophers, of course, would say that consciousness arises in the brain and not in the heart. With due deference to Scientists and Physiologists, it must be stated that, although their investigations and researches more or less definitely have located different centres in the brain as controlling certain phenomena, and though the functions of the brain, which constitute the cerebrum and cerebellum, medulla oblongata and spinal cord, sensory and motor nerves and so on have been understood, which are incontrovertible facts, they have not reached the climax nor would they ever, as their knowledge is not perfect and that knowledge too is with regard to only physical matter. Even in the event of Scientists and Physiologists arriving at the ultimate truth with regard to their findings, they could do so with matter only, but not with immaterial qualities such as consciousness and their mental concomitants, which could be discerned only by an Omniscient. It would be impossible, for instance, for one with worldly knowledge to contrive some appliance or method by which the time taken in a process of thought could be ascertained. The commentators who have gained supra-mundane knowledge and Enlightenment state that a thought process consists of seventeen thought moments, each of which consists of three phases, nascent, static and cessant, whenever a visual object is seen by the eye and before the meaning of the object is understood three other processes arising through the mind-door take place. Each thought moment is supposed to be between one billionth and two billionth part of the time taken in snapping one's fingers or the winking of an eye. Now, phenomena of this nature, which take place from the moment of conception up to death, could only be expounded by the Enlightened Ones, and could never be explained by Chemists, Scientists Physiologists and Philosophers who possess only worldly knowledge.

Buddhism does not deny by any means the truth of their findings; on the other hand, their findings are absolutely in conformity with the doctrine preached by the Buddha, but they have not been able to get at the ultimate and highest truth and to reveal things as they in reality are. Hence, they say that consciousness arises in the brain.

Some allege that the commentators have not described the heart and its contents as they truly are viz. that the heart consists of two auricles and two ventricles and that venous blood comes into the right side of the heart which is pumped out into the lungs and after aeration becomes arterial and so on. The commentators are not concerned with the anatomy and physiology of the heart or any other organ. They say there is a cavity in the heart which contains blood with which is associated the heart-base. The blood is said to be assuming different colours according to the type of consciousness that arises, and this truth is also repudiated by certain critics who are acquainted with the fact that the venous blood is darker than the arterial. No one would deny that venous blood is dark and arterial blood is red. Those conditions are discerned by the naked eye, but the eye of wisdom is necessary to believe in the truth of the fact that different colours are assumed by the blood when influenced by certain classes of consciousness.

The heart-base is neither the heart nor the brain. It is only a material quality derived from the four great essentials and originated from Kamma, which is associated with the blood in the circulation, which is carried on by the heart receiving nerve supply from the brain.

different colours are assumed by the blood when influenced by certain classes of consciousness.

The heart-base is neither the heart nor the brain. It is only a material quality derived from the four great essentials and produced from Kamma, which is associated with the blood in the circulation which is carried on by the heart, receiving nerve supply from the brain.